MW01029495

Building Ballet Technique
Teaching Pointe

By Marilyn Z. Gaston

This book is dedicated to Merrilee Smith

who, during her lifetime, taught diligently as a director of the Atlanta Ballet School, and who will be remembered for many years as a dedicated and devoted ballet instructor who inspired the love of dance in her students and passed on her dedication to the beautiful art of ballet to them.

TABLE OF CONTENTS

Teaching Pointe

Preface

What little girl doesn't dream of wearing those lovely pink satin shoes with ribbons and dancing on her toes? For most, dancing on the toes (or in French, "sur les pointes" or "en pointe") is a strong motivation to continue on with ballet technique classes until that goal is reached.

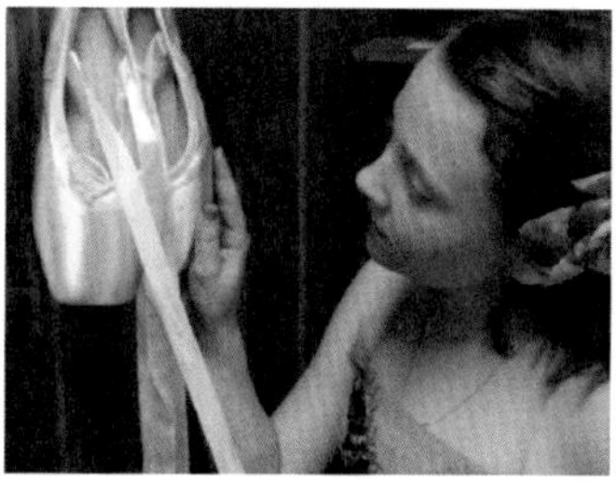

It is often a rude awakening for students to discover how difficult it is to make something so beautiful appear effortless, when, in fact, it requires years of dedicated training both before and after they finally don that first pair of pretty pointe shoes. For some students it is a determining factor as to whether or not they forge onward and upward in their ballet training. It is often an epiphany of sorts, a dividing line that distinguishes the serious student from recreational or hobby dancer. In the world of classical dance it is a "coming-of-age" experience.

As teachers, it is important to prepare students sufficiently so that pointe work does not seem like an insurmountable challenge. It is not simply a matter of wearing the shoes and immediately being able to perform off-pointe steps suddenly "en pointe." They must re-learn much of what they have already accomplished. Teachers must not expect the students to teach themselves or prepare themselves without guidance. Just allowing them to wear pointe shoes in a regular ballet technique class does not produce the necessary result, and often causes students to become frustrated. *Correct teaching of pointe separately in specialized lessons is essential.* It often means regressing to slower and more focused work—back to the barre, in fact—and can be discouraging to dancers already accustomed to doing certain steps with ease in soft shoes.

But if students are adequately strengthened and given a deliberate and careful approach by teaching within certain limits they will progress slowly but surely towards their goal of becoming as proficient on pointe as they previously were in soft ballet shoes alone. It is vital that they be given correct preparatory work, and later given beginning work that does not exceed their physical or chronological age and growth capabilities. There is no "fast food" approach to this goal! Even the most talented child endowed with so-called "perfect feet" for pointe must be nurtured and not rushed into advanced-level work too early. To do so may cause irreparable damage that may not appear until later in life, including back, ankle and foot injuries.

The foundational training is everything in dance. It is so much more rewarding in the end to teach with realistic expectations from your students. The responsibility is entirely yours to prepare them, nurture them, and design class work that makes pointe seem not only possible, but exciting and enjoyable. Likewise, teachers need to be aware of how to teach pointe work to students with less-than-perfect (as perhaps defined by strictest ballet standards) physical gifts. They, too, can learn to do well and may surprise you with their dedication and determination. You, as a teacher, should be able to analyze and guide them towards achievement. Advanced students should be presented with challenging work that leads them towards performing both classical and contemporary choreography by introducing them to solo and group variations from the well-known ballets they may be asked to perform in auditions, competitions, and on stage as professional company members.

Each one of the sample classes and exercises presented here are just that—samples. As a teacher you may adapt them to your own style and approach. However, the pace and level of difficulty suggested will give you an idea as to the progression of teaching pointe.

This book is intended to address that need, and to provide guidelines for teachers, both experienced and novice, to utilize when preparing students for pointe work and continuing that training through years of careful classroom exercises until it culminates in rehearsing classical repertoire and experiencing partnering while *en pointe*.

My first volume in this series (*Building Ballet Technique, A Practical Guide to Teaching All Levels*) touched upon this subject in a single chapter, and now it is time to explore it in more depth and with a more customized approach. Because it is so vital to teaching pointe I have decided to reiterate some of that material throughout this volume as excerpts in various chapters. Likewise I have drawn from my own written thesis material *(Ballet Pedagogy: A Conceptual Approach*) now on file at the Fine Arts library, University of Oklahoma.

If you are new to teaching, even after years of taking classes and perhaps a performing career yourself, it is hoped that this book will prove helpful towards your continued success in inspiring your students to become accomplished artists in this uniquely beautiful classical form of ballet.

NOTE: As in all books from this series, ballet terms used here are in italics. If you are uncertain about terminology, please consult Gail Grant's excellent reference book, *Technical Manual and Dictionary of Classical Ballet.* A brief Glossary of Terms as used in the sample lesson plans within these pages is also included in the back of this volume.

Chapter One

Teacher's evaluation of students for pointe work

Before allowing a student to go on pointe, there are certain criteria to consider as a way of determining whether or not a student is ready. Pre-pointe classes automatically give the invited students the expectation of continuing on to eventually join a pointe class, so it is important to be consistent when deciding which students you will include in the class.

Here are some suggested student assessment considerations for teachers to consider when determining which students are ready to begin pointe work:

1. *Age:*

- Most teachers agree that age is less important than physical development and training, but also that the stress put upon bones, ligaments, tendons and muscles should preclude starting children on pointe before age 10 at the earliest.
- Most teachers would agree that age 11 to 13 or even later is more appropriate.

2. *Physicality:*

- Other considerations include strength, placement, coordination and foot/ankle structure. Sometimes the outward appearance of a student is deceptive; a small, fragile body may in fact be better suited than a stocky body because the skeleton and muscles are supporting a lighter weight.

- The foot structure may discourage any pointe work—sometimes the arch is flat and (if the student has been observed for some years beforehand in regular technique classes) shows no sign of being able to achieve more flexibility, or the ankle is too stiff to enable the student's foot to fully stretch. This is even more important than the formation of the leg itself—legs that are bowed or hyperextended or with knees that do not fully "pull up" may be able to change over time with careful training and a strong desire on the part of the student. The foot and ankle, however, if not showing signs of improvement over time, even with sincere effort on the part of both teacher and student, may be unable to change. Students who sickle the foot repeatedly in *tendu* or other exercises should be corrected until the problem disappears. A student who cannot *demi-plié* without lifting the heels from the floor has short tendons and this will also inhibit success in performing on pointe.

- As a teacher, it is your responsibility to advise students who have, for example, a very long big toe with other toes all shorter—this student will be putting almost all of the weight upon that toe to dance on pointe and will need a shoe to accommodate that length. Conversely, a student bearing majority weight on the smaller middle toes must be sure to develop enough metatarsal strength to do so.

- A student with very flexible, high arches may have a different challenge. This is a foot that looks quite beautiful on pointe, but often is not strong either in the ankles or arch or metatarsals. Extra care should be given to make sure students do not "roll over" the toes too far, but should be instructed to feel ι they "pull the foot up out of the shoe" when goi. up on pointe.

3. *Psychological temperament:*

- Often overlooked, it is a teacher's responsibility to consider the student's motivation and dedication before allowing pointe work. Many students find early pointe exercises to be painful or become depressed when the difficulty and long-term commitment necessary for success is apparent. Some students may not be emotionally capable of subjecting themselves to the increased level of difficulty required.

4. *Number of classes taken per week and years of previous study:*

- A student being considered for pointe, if meeting the other requirements, should ideally be taking at least three dedicated ballet technique classes per week, and should have been taking at least 2-3 classes weekly for the previous two years. More is always better.

- Additionally, it is assumed that the student has been studying ballet with a competent teacher for the past 2-3 years, minimum, excluding Creative Movement, Pre-Ballet or Primary levels.

5. *Studio physical equipment requirements:*

- The floor of a dance studio is of prime importance when teaching pointe, as well as any other dance form, particularly ballet technique. It should be a resilient floor that is constructed with materials that provide a softer surface than cement or very hard wood with no "give" to it. Older flooring is often already constructed with an air surface underneath, mounting the subflooring upon a layer of "basket weave" beams, but newer floors are often (unfortunately for the dancer) made of cement or poured concrete as a foundation. In this case the studio should purchase or build a raised flooring surface that provides a "cushion" beneath the danceable surface.

For details, consult the Internet for dance flooring that is already pre-constructed and meant to be laid in sections directly upon the subfloor of cement, or for directions about how to construct a proper floor. The impact of a dancer when landing jumps or coming down from a *relevé* on pointe is a very important consideration; injuries often result from ignoring this important aspect of dance studio equipment, and many such injuries may not show up until later in a dancer's life.

- The surface of the floor must provide enough traction to keep pointe shoes from slipping, considering the surface contacting the floor when on pointe at the end of the shoe tip is satin—a very slippery material. Earlier, dancers often darned (sewed threads across the tip of the toes repeatedly—see Chapter 2) that would absorb rosin (a sticky substance in "rock" form that serves as hardened glue to give "tackiness" to a shoe; gymnasts use this in powdered form on their hands) to accomplish this, and some dancers still perform this ritual. It is also a way to preserve the toe shoe so that the satin does not shred or fall off the end of the shoe, and the toe box remains intact longer.

Today we have stage floor covering that gives the ballet dancer confidence because it provides a non-slick surface, unlike linoleum or bare wood. This comes in many forms and is rolled out and taped down on top of the "floating floor" surface of a studio. It has many brand names and is often called "marley" as a generic term—it was originally a rubberized surface used on ship decks to give traction to sailors at sea! Again, consult the Internet—various manufacturers supply this. While expensive, it is well worth the price to avoid injuries from falls that might occur without it.

Warning signs that a student is not ready for pointe work:

- A student with very weak ankles who cannot sustain a *relevé* position correctly on two feet in either soft ballet shoes or on pointe without wobbling or rolling (pronating) or supranating (rolling outward) is not yet ready. The student should also be able to reach this position while doing "spring *relevés*" (Cecchetti *relevés*). Students should be able to do these multiple times at the barre and in the center floor in soft shoes first.

- A student who is not putting weight on all toes when standing on the balls of the feet needs further work. If the student is clutching the toes, further work is needed to encourage relaxing the metatarsals and using the top of the arch with toes extended. One of the best ways to assess this is to have students take off their shoes and make the student aware of the difference. Often, with young students, having them walk on half-toe across the floor will discourage this from occurring later.

- The student should be able to stand on a high 3/4 pointe position in soft shoes with the knees "lifted," the torso upright, the placement correct in the spine (no swaying of the back, or tucking under of the pelvis, or bending the knees). Students unable to reach a high position due to stiff ankles may improve over time, unless the problem is a physical one that will not change.

FAQ about teaching pointe that may arise:

What about adult ballet students taking pointe?

- When teaching I have often been asked by adult students whether or not they could take pointe class. Often they are motivated by a desire to experience the "ultimate" goal of taking ballet classes. On the rare occasion that I have allowed this for adults, I have made the following stipulations: (1) they must be taking regular ballet technique classes at least 3-4 times per week, and have been doing that regimen for at least three recent years with steady attendance; (2) they must have reasonable body weight according to their height—an overweight adult might be liable to put dangerous stress upon ankles, feet and metatarsals, or conversely, a very underweight adult may have insufficient muscular development to sustain pointe work; (3) they should have enough arch and ankle flexibility to ensure they will be able to reach a full pointe position; and (4) they should be willing to make a commitment towards at least a 10-week session or an entire semester of pointe classes, since a too-short exposure will not allow them to pass beyond the initial, and possible unexpected, difficulty of beginner exercises. Most are duly surprised by the effort required to do even the simplest moves in pointe shoes versus soft shoes. I have found that once their curiosity is satisfied, most adult students do not continue on with pointe work.

- I have also been asked to teach pointe to college dancers who are majoring in dance, perhaps with an emphasis on modern technique, who may had little or no exposure to pointe work, or are considered to be at a beginning level in their ballet technique. Pointe work encountered at this age in either case does not have the final goal of developing students who can perform on pointe. Rather, the goal is to give students the *experience* of pointe as an adjunct to their overall dance knowledge. They should usually be expected to have sufficient strength and placement ability that would enable a successful beginning achievement level on pointe and be taught the basics of pedagogy that should be applied to pointe in the event they are one day called upon to teach it. A minimum of three ballet classes per week should be required, preferably more.

What about male students who want to try pointe?

- Male dance students often express an interest in pointe as something they feel will enhance their foot position, make their feet more flexible, or simply give them an idea of what it is like to dance on pointe if they anticipate teaching pointe classes in the future. The same guidelines apply here regarding age if they are under 18 years old. Otherwise, adult males may be allowed to experience pointe short-term and carefully supervised *at the teacher's discretion*, in a separate class situation from female students. However, if the male dancer cannot achieve a full pointe position, i.e., they either clutch the toes to accomplish it or have stiff ankles that do not accommodate a fully arched foot, they will find pointe work very tedious so teachers should be aware that the physcical strength they otherwise have does not necessarily compensate for the lack of flexibility needed in the foot and ankle.

My personal belief, perhaps not shared by other teachers, is that male dancers do not need to actually dance on pointe in order to teach pointe. However, they should definitely be aware of good-versus-poor pointe work as it applies to female students, particularly if they are teaching partnering or plan to choreograph pointe pieces for female dancers. Most of the time male teachers absorb this knowledge by being in classes themselves as students where they observe their female counterparts dancing on pointe. A male teacher should not wear pointe shoes as a demonstrator when teaching, as the male foot is often of a different construction anatomically than that of a female. Students copy their teachers.

- Male teachers should be aware that some movements are unrealistic or impossible, or even dangerous when performed in toe shoes as opposed to soft shoes or bare feet. Likewise, dancers on pointe turn faster when partnered, and have certain limitations imposed by the shoes when it comes to control and balance.

Is it necessary for the teacher to wear pointe shoes herself when teaching pointe?

- No. A verbal explanation of proper position on pointe, and using a student to demonstrate is sufficient. The students should watch each other and listen to the teacher and not be dependent upon the teacher to "perform" for them.

- Giving constant and close attention through corrections to students, especially in the first months of lessons should serve to correct any problems. Observe them carefully and be encouraging at all times. Pointe is like learning to dance all over again in many ways; give them time to master the basics before expecting to see them "comfortable" on pointe overnight!

A final word...

There are, sadly, some students who should never even attempt pointe—and often teachers will allow them to go on pointe anyway due to parental pressure or the desire to accommodate their need to stay within the same class grouping. These students suffer the frustration of wondering why some of their colleagues find pointe work fun and challenging while they may find it almost tortuous. This is where a responsible teacher should steer the student towards a non-pointe idiom in dance so that they can still enjoy and use what they have learned without feeling overwhelmed—or suggest they remain with their group but do not participate on pointe. Often a student will come to this conclusion themselves, but if allowed to become too discouraged, will then quit dancing altogether, which I see as an unfortunate outcome.

Chapter Two

The Evolution of Pointe and the Pointe Shoe Deconstructed

For nearly two centuries, female ballet dancers wore only soft shoes made of cloth, with thin ribbons attached to keep them on their feet while jumping or rising from the floor. Even these were an improvement over the earliest shoes from the time of court ballet, which were hard-heeled and based upon street shoes worn by the aristocracy. Leather and cloth shoes made it possible to flex the arches, but at the price of giving less protection to the foot.

While there is still some discussion about which ballerinas were the initiators to perform on pointe, most historians agree that the first well-known ballerina to rise onto her toes was Marie Taglioni, in 1832. She was in fact the first to dance an entire ballet wearing pointe shoes (*La Sylphide*) and this innovation was rapidly adopted by other ballerinas until it became the norm for female classical dancers.

Marie Taglioni

Her strength must have been phenomenal considering the first pointe shoes were simply soft ballet shoes with the toes reinforced by darning (sewing threads back and forth across the toe tips) and with little stiffening of the shanks (soles) or toe box that now characterize the modern pointe shoe. The shoe was modeled somewhat after the "street shoe" of the time, with a full-length sole that inhibited bending of the arch. Imagine dancing on the toes while wearing, essentially, stiff cloth socks with some layers of thread sewn across the toes! Eventually the shoes evolved into a reinforced full-length shank and stiff box at the toe, but with little consideration given to the realistic shape of a human foot; rather, the early shoes were narrow and straight and far too inflexible to allow for a beautiful arch.

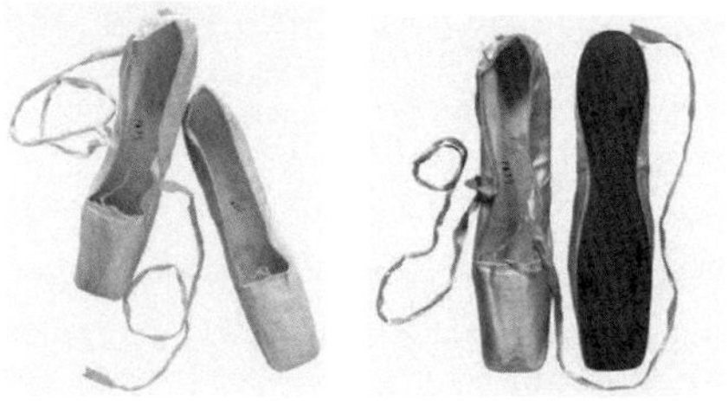

Examples of early pointe shoes

◄

Of course, dancers were not then expected to perform the technical virtuoso steps on pointe that are required of today's classical ballerinas. One assumes that the occasional *piqué arabesque* or *bourrée* done *en pointe* at that time would have astounded the audiences. Typically, in the era of the Romantic ballet, ballerinas were highly competitive and this new "gimmick" quickly introduced an element that soon became the hallmark of female dancers everywhere. Choreographers constantly challenged the dancers to perform new feats of ability to show off this innovation in the ballet world. They soon discovered that pointe work facilitated partnering by giving the ballerina added height to match that of her male counterpart, and made certain moves in partnering (*promenade, pirouettes*, etc.) far easier to execute since she now had less resistance to the floor. Costume skirts were shortened to show the foot.

Needless to say, pointe work required far more strength and balance than working in soft shoes which only required rising to the balls of the feet. Female dancers now had to readjust their center of balance, learn to control turns at a higher speed, and be able to jump while wearing heavier footwear. Training dancers to work on pointe became an essential part of the ballet teacher's regimen, and demanded extra teaching time and a full knowledge of guiding students towards the successful, injury-free accomplishment of a difficult skill.

With its creation, the toe shoes worn by dancers were constantly adapted to the increased technical skills, and that evolution continues to this day. Pointe shoe manufacturers are eternally searching for a new, more appealing shoe "model" that will entice dancers to try their products. Dancers are often willing to try new brands and designs in an effort to enhance their comfort and performance. Makers tout their improvements to keep sales brisk, and consequently shoes have become quite expensive considering their short "shelf life" and the need for constant replacement.

For professional performers in a ballet company, shoes are provided at the expense of the company—otherwise the dancers' entire salaries would be spent on pointe shoes! For students, the expense falls upon their parents or themselves, and can often be daunting. In either case, dancers themselves must learn to sew ribbons and elastics onto the shoes by hand, a process that becomes part of their pointe shoe experience.

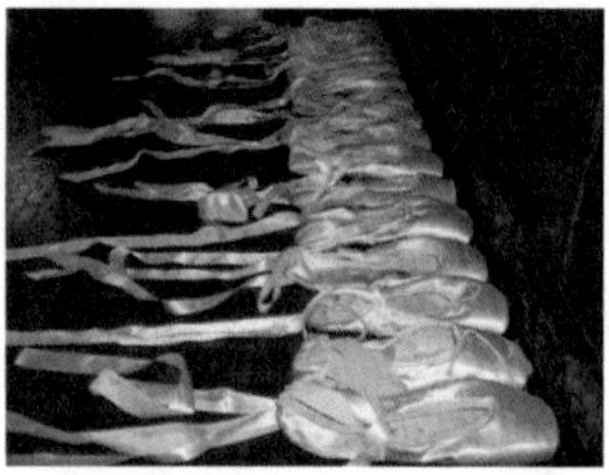

It is not unusual for a professional dancer to use a pair of shoes every other week!

◄

Today's dancers demand a more comfortable shoe, with a broader, stiffer box at the front giving better lateral balance, and a flatter, shorter vamp to conform to the shape of the dancer's toes. The shank, or sole of the shoe, has been made slimmer and cut down at the heel area to allow for ease of rising and lowering through the shoe while still giving adequate support to the foot, thus allowing for a more flexible arch, silent shoe, and roll-through ability.

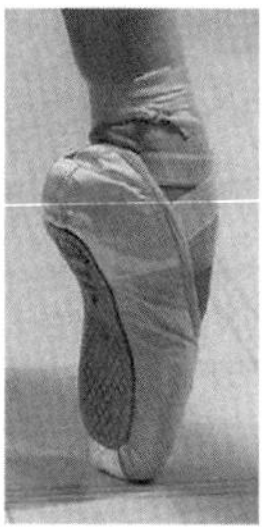

The modern pointe shoe. Note 3/4 shank and wider box

◄

With the constantly changing shoe designs and more difficult technical requirements for dancers, it became necessary for all female classical dancers to receive specialized training for pointe work, and for teachers to include this as part of their instruction. Teachers must be careful observers and adaptors, always able to know (sense) when and what to give beginners, especially, and how to customize the work to suit each individual physical capability and student skill set.

The Pointe Shoe Deconstructed

Before going forward with descriptions of exercises and lesson plans for pre-pointe and pointe, it is a good idea to educate both students and parents about toe shoes, especially if they will be going with their child to buy their first pair of shoes. If the teacher is unable to attend the fittings (often the case if schedules are incompatible), be sure to disseminate this information beforehand. Best to put it in a written handout, if possible.

Stress that the student must not wear or soil the shoes until the teacher has subsequently checked the fit and style of the shoes and that, if they ignore this important fact, they may end up having to return to the store to exchange them—and worn shoes, even slightly, will usually not be accepted for exchange or refund. Make an additional note about ribbons and elastic you prefer as well as any "accessories" such as toe pads, lamb's wool, toe tape, and so on.

A personal note here is that I often find students and parents rush to the store as soon as they know their child will be allowed to attend a pointe class—often without heeding this advice. Be adamant in your warnings about this because the child will be greatly disappointed if she finds out her shoes are not acceptable, and the parent will be equally displeased when they need to return to the store a second time, or are denied a refund or exchange. Stress also that shoes are not fitted to same size as street shoes, and they should never order a pair online without trying them on unless it is the same style and size as they are accustomed to wearing previously.

What are the parts of a pointe shoe called?

This is information you may want to disperse to parents of beginner pointe students. The undersole of the shoe is referred to as the **shank**. It is usually made of leather. Shanks are usually graded as "soft, medium or hard." The shank does not (should not) cover the heel portion of the shoe as it would in a street shoe. The front, hardened part of the shoe covering the toes (achieved by layering paper maché and glue, or in some newer shoes, by man-made fiber materials) is the **box**. It is meant to break down and soften with wear and will become more comfortable, and usually "flatten" over the toes as the shoes are worn. Sides of the box/shoe are referred to as the **wings**. The **vamp** is the length area of the box, though shoes may be sized by both the length and width of the box. A longer vamp is needed for longer toes, usually, or a foot with a high arch; a shorter box provides less support underneath the metatarsals and provides an easier "roll through" when descending off pointe and is suitable for a low-to-medium arch and/or shorter toes. When trying on shoes, the foot should not "fall" into the box; rather the shoe should be encouraging the student to lift up "out of the shoe" when on pointe.

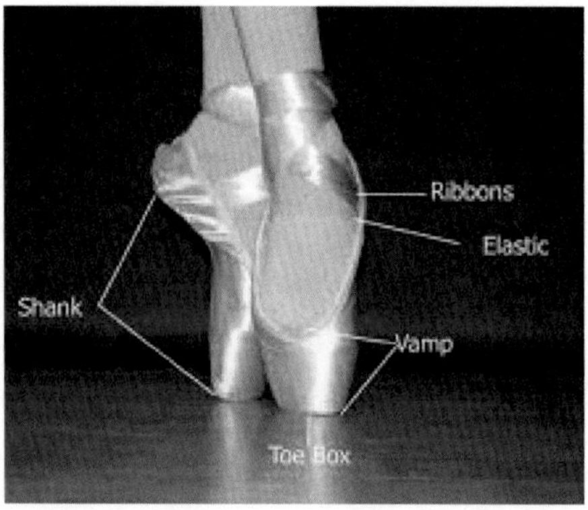

When fitting, care should be given to providing the student with the proper length, width and hardness of the shank. In general, a weaker or high-arched foot needs a harder shank than a stronger or low-arched foot or a well-developed, strongly-arched, professional foot. Beginners should look for these unless they have a low-arched foot with less arch or ankle flexibility, in which case they will need a medium shank. A professional shoe, often called a performance shoe, is easy to break in quickly and can often be used on short notice for a performance, but is often not suitable for a student dancer who will then need new shoes too often, or who needs a shoe with more support for the foot.

What are guidelines for fitting shoes and advising students of the proper fit and sewing and tying of pointe shoes? There are so many brands now that it is hard to know how to advise students.

Without trying on shoes themselves, teachers can only advise students after seeing them try the brands on their own feet. Brand descriptions are usually not helpful, as manufacturers want their shoes to appeal to the widest possible buying public. At best they may make a reference to "suitable for the advanced dancer" but rarely do they provide a specific guideline. Shoemakers continue to expand their style offerings so that dancers will ultimately continue to experiment and thus buy the latest, newest shoe in their endless quest for the "perfect pointe shoe." Professionals, on the other hand, usually find a shoe that works for them and will re-order that shoe consistently as long as it is made. They have neither the time nor inclination to request that the company or theatre ordering their shoes constantly change vendors.

I believe it would be helpful if shoe styles were defined in more detailed terms, but doubt that will ever happen. Perhaps a chart of some kind could be offered that describes certain typical foot characteristics and then shoes could be rated according to how well they address those. Thus a dancer with a long big toe and low, flat arch and narrow heel could try to match those characteristics with a shoe that purports to be suitable. A dancer with a high arch, long middle toes, and a wide, short foot construction would look for a different style that the manufacturer might claim is specific to those definitions. This would seem much more valuable than the current method of description that often simply states "long vamp, medium shank," etc. As it stands now, the only viable way to find the perfect shoe is through trial and error—and that can be costly. **Store owners or clerks cannot always be relied upon to provide the correct shoe or even fit of the shoe, as many are interested only in selling the student something before they leave the building!** And few store owners or clerks have been dancers themselves, or may have had less-than-reliable training in the area, though they may present themselves as experts. Some do not want to spend the necessary time with students and/or their teachers to find (especially) a first pair of shoes for a beginner that works best for them. Some do know their jobs well, however; ask other students for references, or ask if your school recommends a particular vendor. Be sure to advise your students about ribbons you, the teacher, may prefer, elastics, toe pads, etc. and/or the various "accessories" that the store may promote, but may not be necessary and are just extra expenses. Be sure students try on shoes wearing the toe pads or other accessories they will be using.

Teachers should accompany students on their first trip for shoes—or have the store owner bring a variety of styles and sizes (sometimes not a practical possibility) to the studio for a fitting. Beginners should be advised not to buy online for their first pair, in any case. Online sizing charts are only estimates, and since the beginner is unaccustomed to how toe shoes feel upon first wearing and sizing varies according to brand, they are unlikely to know when they have found a good fit or style.

Sewing shoes is, I find, often the earliest duty of parents, not students. Though students should be encouraged to do it themselves from the onset, I find that many will leave it to their mothers. Therefore I usually brought the parents into the studio and showed them a pair of shoes properly sewn and gave them a step-by-step instruction sheet as well. If they told me they did not know how to sew by hand I would encourage them to practice on a scrap of cloth. One can only advise, in the hope that they will take pride in learning how to do it and quickly teach their children to take over the job. Rarely do "hired tailors" do this job correctly, though they may happily charge exorbitant fees for their efforts. I try to impress upon students that this is a "special" duty that professional dancers all learn to do—hoping that will give them the incentive to learn.

It should be emphasized to all students and parents that this is a *hand-sewing job*; machine sewing is NOT effective and often results in ribbons or elastics coming loose from the shoe. Advise students never to use safety pins to procure ribbons or elastics because there is too much tension, and if the pin opens the dancers will be injured.

Tying shoes is often best taught when students are still in soft ballet shoes—thus they have the ribbons sewn and tied onto their soft shoes for a year prior to going on pointe. Often the students see this as a "graduation" and if it can be taught before the pointe shoes arrive—so much the better. There is a difference, of course, insofar as they will not be sewing on elastics yet or putting the ribbons in the exact same reference points as one uses for pointe shoes, but it is a start. Note that the final knot should be tucked in under the crossed ribbons *on the inside of the ankle* and not visibly apparent when the tying is done.

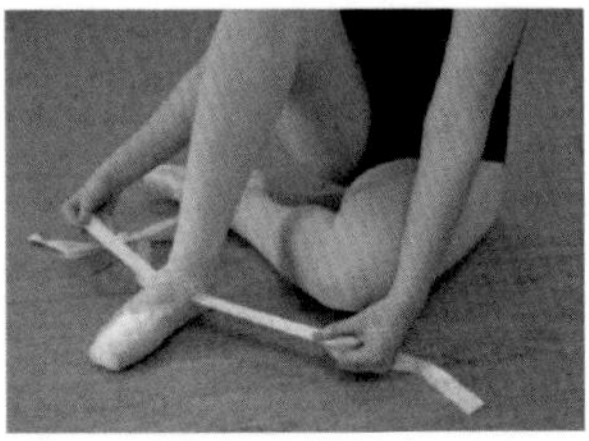

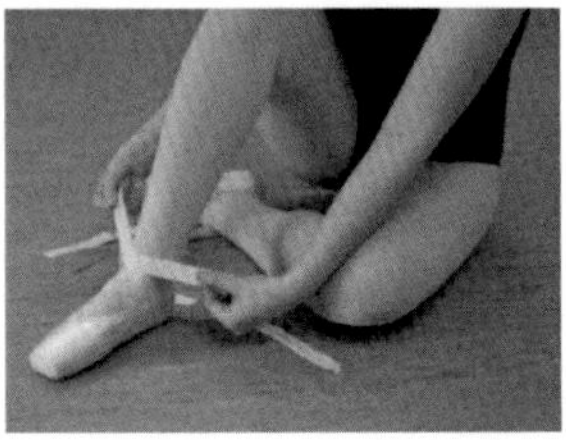

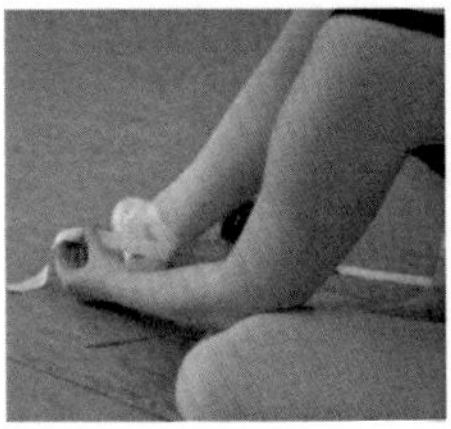

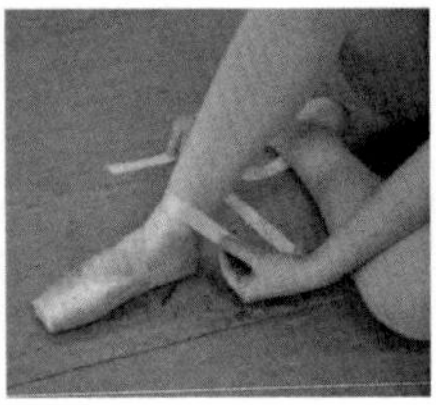

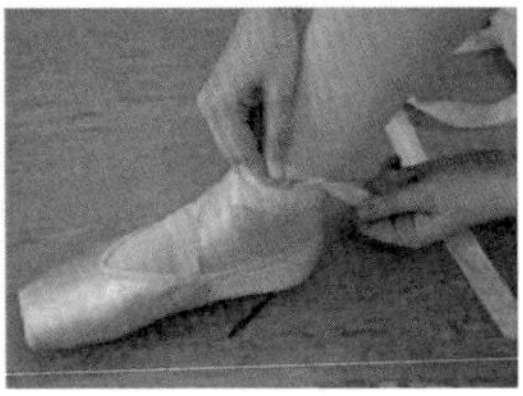

Darning shoes is usually not necessary, but it does protect the satin tips from shredding and may make the box last longer since it cushions the ends somewhat. The main purpose of darning used to be that it provided traction by adding a layer of threads for absorbing rosin when dancers were performing on bare wood or on slippery surfaces. Today, with the advent of rubberized stage flooring that equips most studios and stages, it is often unnecessary.

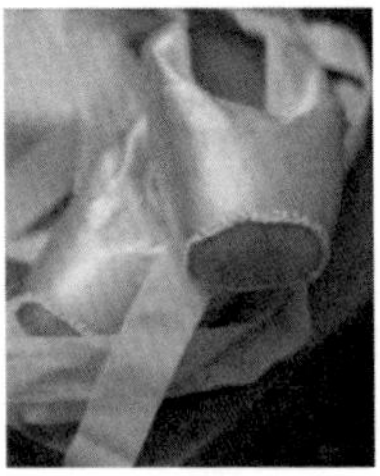

Darning pointe shoes, the beginning ◄

the finished job ►

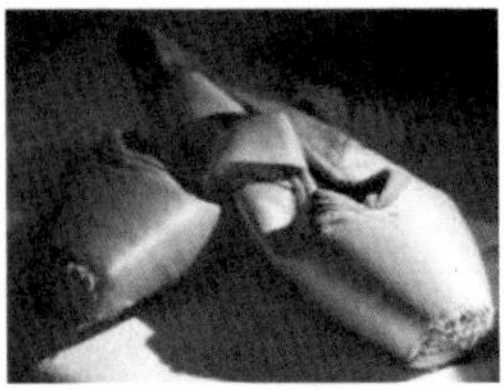

The darning process begins by sewing a circular pattern of stitching around and around the toe surface (see above). It should protrude slightly away from the shoe, with stitches anchored into the shoe satin. Then stitches should be made in a straight line across the circle horizontally, occasionally (in this initial work) anchoring into the shoe satin. After going back and forth across horizontally, then do the same vertically, creating a "checkerboard" effect. Lines should be about a quarter-inch apart. Continue sewing, alternating horizontal sets of lines with vertical sets; as the thread "pad" develops, the threads will be anchored to each other until there is a build-up of the surface by several or more layers of threads. (see "the finished job" above). Remember that the dancer must still be able to "feel" the floor.

Should pointe work be included in a "regular" ballet technique class as opposed to being given in a separate pointe class)?

A structured pointe class is necessary for students whose feet and ankles need strengthening or who are beginning on pointe and need constant monitoring to be sure bad habits do not develop. *If a student is a non-professional, it is essential that they have some dedicated pointe classes that deal specifically with the demands of pointe work, demands that differ from those normally found in a non-pointe ballet technique class alone.*

A regular ballet technique class taken while wearing pointe shoes has some benefits, and some drawbacks. Among the benefits are strengthening the feet and ankles, becoming accustomed to wearing pointe shoes while jumping and doing connecting (off-pointe) steps, and perhaps developing the extra balance references needed when performing *promenades* and other adagio steps with the challenge of working in a rounded and more rigid shoe box. The ability to walk, run, land jumps, and complete *terre-à-terre* steps such as *glissade* soundlessly in pointe shoes often shows improvement in a technique class situation.

There are also drawbacks, which can sometimes inhibit a dancer, particularly a non-professional dancer. Working in soft ballet shoes gives a better "feel" for the floor that needs to be established during *demi-pliés* and landing jumps, and even in walking and running steps. This has to be learned first in ballet shoes in order to "translate" later into pointe work. Without feeling the floor fully a student can often exhibit a less-than-complete use of the foot because the foot is necessarily restricted during certain movements within a pointe shoe. The 3/4 pointe position is difficult to maintain and hold while wearing pointe shoes; dancers "go through" this position to rise and lower from pointe, of course, but are rarely asked to hold it while in pointe shoes since the stiff shank often prevents it. It needs to be practiced in soft shoes for students to be able to find a high half-pointe position on the balls of the feet.

From a teaching point of view, I think students should only be allowed to take technique classes wearing pointe shoes after they have achieved a high intermediate-to-advanced level of technique—and should not take every class entirely in pointe shoes. Occasionally it is necessary to dance onstage in soft shoes or even bare feet—so thought must be given to working sufficiently without the extra support and restriction provided by pointe shoes.

However professionals and others who are asked to rehearse on pointe several hours daily or perform nightly on pointe (or both) usually refrain from taking every ballet company class on pointe, partially because pointe shoes must be "saved" for those more important activities, and also because too much pointe work can sometimes result in shorter tendons and tighter calf muscles, ultimately ending in less elevation and a heightened chance for injury.

Taping, Padding & Pointe Shoe Accessories

In addition to ribbons and elastics, there are other necessities that the student or teacher may encourage students to use. One of these is padding, and it is rarely an "optional" addition to the dancer's footwear. Originally dancers used combed lamb's wool—a soft, recycleable natural product that could be divided into small or larger portions as needed, wrapped around the toes, and used to cushion the foot from the rigid shoe box and hard floor. When it eventually "balls up" it can be manipulated by hand by pulling gently at it until the fibers loosen and then re-shaped. While it is somewhat out of fashion currently, it is still available and is reasonably priced.

For those who wish a more trendy form of padding there are gel and foam pads, even perhaps still "bunny fur" lined pads. The problem with gel pads is that when pressure is applied to the gel it moves—thus when the toes press downward against it, the gel may shift sideways and leave the tips of the toes or knuckles exposed. Often it does not allow the foot to "breathe" either—air does not penetrate the vinyl lined padding which is unhealthy for the skin. Foam pads can bunch up or crumble, or, at the very least, retain odor. Their biggest "plus" is that they are washable. Bunny fur pads are often too bulky. In any case, strive to make the padding as invisible as possible—it should not show or stick out of the front of the shoe. With the advent of "convertible" tights (highly recommended) the dancer can place the pads underneath the toe of the tights which solves this problem.

More optional, and perhaps only considered with the teacher's permission or advice, are devices such as "toe spacers." These, (it is thought) when inserted between the big toe and adjacent toe, keep the toes "aligned" and help prevent "hammer toe"—a condition in which the big toe permanently "leans" towards the second toe, or bunions, an enlargement of the big toe as a result of pressure on the outside of the base of the toe. They are usually made of clear or white vinyl, slightly flexible, and may come in sizes. Personally I believe one should be careful in using them—some foot structures do not need them and may even be held out of alignment by them. Seek your teacher's advice before investing in them. Above all, it is important to "feel" the floor for balance and traction.

To avoid blisters, try taping the tender areas such as the knuckles of the toes. Tape each one individually using a breatheable tape such as cloth tape that is painless to remove.

Watch out for….

- *Bruises.* Usually these are the result of impact, but may also occur from too-tight shoes, or a particular pressure point within the shoe against the foot that needs attention. If a bruise does not clear up with the use of ice or within a short time, investigate the latter possibility. In the interim, use extra padding over the painful area. Bruised toe nails can be especially difficult; if the bruise persists the toe nail may fall off. Keep it clean and well-padded.

- *Blisters.* These are common among pointe shoe wearers and begin by a rubbing off of skin where there is a pressure point. If you are able to catch this early reddening stage, clean the affected area and put extra padding and a bandage over the spot. If, however, the skin is broken or a blister appears above the reddened area, it is very important to clean it immediately, stop any bleeding, and protect the area from further irritation and infection. Using alcohol or hydrogen peroxide frequently will help the blister itself dry up and eventually drop off. Meantime, pad well and bandage. Soaking may be soothing but may keep the skin from drying up and healing if it is kept constantly moist.

- *Calluses.* These are rough, scaly patches of skin that form to protect the skin underneath. Often they have less feeling than the surrounding skin. With dancers they most often occur on the balls of the feet (from turns) or heels. While they may be uncomfortable, be careful about removing them or peeling the outer layer of skin off. The skin underneath will be very tender "new" skin, very sensitive and may be unable to withstand contact. Remove the callus gently with a file or by soaking rather than by battery-operated machine or peeling.

- *Ingrown toe nails*. Ouch! These hurt. This is when the sharp edge of the nail, often the big toe, digs into (grows into) the outer skin surrounding it. Soaking will soften the surrounding skin, and then the skin can be pushed gently back, away from the nail, and the nail trimmed finally. This may take time. This can be avoided if the nails are trimmed regularly and a small notch is cut into the center of the nail—causing it to "fill in" the notch rather than grow outward into the skin. In extreme cases it may be necessary to consult a podiatrist.

Teach your students how to properly care for their feet and toes by discussing these possiblities and asking them to report any problems to you before they become major issues.

Chapter Three
The Pre-Pointe Class

Why Pre-Pointe?

Parents often wonder why a pre-pointe class is necessary when their daughters have already spent years in regular technique classes, or how pre-pointe differs from beginning pointe. As teachers, we should distinguish this as a separate lesson plan and put emphasis upon certain aspects of technique that will increase a student's success when they finally begin actual pointe classes. So the term "pre-pointe" refers to preparatory classes done in regular ballet soft shoes prior to actually working in pointe shoes.

If you have a limited number of students it may sometimes be necessary to simply include pre-pointe in a beginning pointe class by allowing some students in the same time slot to do the work in soft shoes until they are deemed ready to wear toe shoes. Others may already be able to do the lessons *en pointe*. Ideally it is better to separate the students by ability and strength rather than have some in soft shoes, some doing pointe work only at barre, and some doing pointe work both at barre and in the center within the same class group. In such a mixed setting, it is difficult for the teacher to adequately observe the varied physiques and spot any problems.

NOTE: Pre-pointe is taught entirely in regular soft ballet shoes—personally, I do not like the "pre-pointe" or "demi-pointe" shoes that have a box-like front and no supportive shank—*students still try to stand on pointe in them, which is dangerous!* What I have always done, however, is have students sew ribbons onto their soft ballet shoes during this pre-pointe year and learn how to tie them before they actually get their first pair of pointe shoes. Then they already know the correct way to do this before they get their pointe shoes.

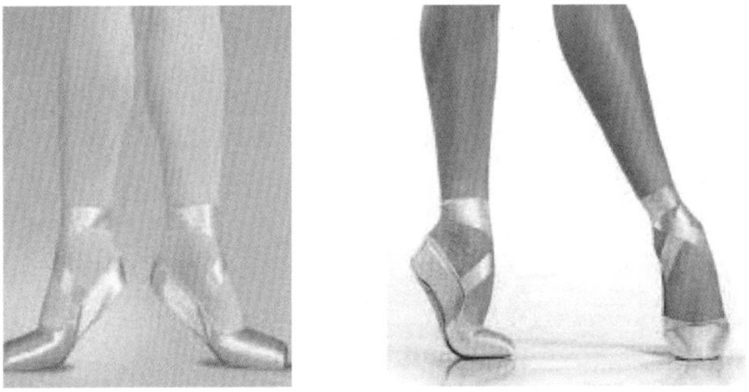

Two views of pre-pointe (demi-pointe) shoes. There is no strong shank or box support for actual pointe work. . ▲

Teachers should follow the natural difficulty level and be sure each level is achieved before introducing the next level. This is: (1) "spring" *relevés* on two feet (*sous-sus, échappé relevé*), (2) one foot to two feet (*assemblé soutenu*), (3) two feet to one foot (*passé relevé, sissonne simple*), and (4) *piqué (pas de bourrée),* walks and runs on pointe (*pas couru*), *bourrée sur place, bourrée* traveling, (5) one foot to same foot (multiple *relevés* in *arabesque, fouetté turns, ballonnées en pointe*, for example), (6) jumps on pointe *(changements)* and (7) hops on one foot on pointe or on same foot successively (polka step, hops in *arabesque*, etc.).

Before using the lesson plans for pointe listed here, check to be sure your students are able to do the following in their regular ballet technique classes before enrolling them in pre-pointe or pointe:

- An increase at barre of *tendues* done at varying tempi should be given. From this, the student should also be able to do *assemblé soutenu* (extend leg to *tendu* in *fondu*, then pull leg sharply back into 5th with both legs straight—later do with pulling up *to sous-sus)*. It is also helpful to do *tendu* with flexes so students stretch the Achilles tendon and feel the separation between metatarsal flex and ankle flex. I find that *battement relevé* (rolling the foot down to flat position, the rolling up to full *tendu)* done slowly is helpful. It is important that this is done with both legs straight, as lifting the knees while rolling down will later become necessary on pointe. Practice of *sous-sus* at barre and in center is important as this is preparing them for "pulling the foot under," i.e., replacing the ball of the foot with the toe when doing a spring *relevé.*

- French *relevés* (sometimes called *élevés*): slow rises without bending the knees from flat position to 3/4 pointe and back down. Done facing the barre, stressing keeping the knees "pulled up" throughout rise and lower, very slowly so that student feels all the levels. Good to combine with *demi-* and *grand pliés* to give calf muscles a change to both contract and release. Later make sure students can lift hands off barre and hold the raised position securely with all toes relaxed and contacting the floor. Check to be sure turnout is maintained and held so inside muscles of the thighs are utilized and heels are kept in line with toes. Each student will have a different degree of turnout; as long as they are working to the fullest extent of their own physical ability, it will be beneficial.

- Cecchetti ("spring") *relevés*. I like to do these referring back to the Royal Academy syllabus of some years ago: facing the barre, the students first practice them in both 1st and 2nd positions separately. Musically, it is syncopated, i.e., the *demi-plié* is on "and" before first count, the "spring" to 3/4 pointe is first count, the HOLD at highest position lasts for count 2-3-4. This is far more beneficial that giving these at "even" counts which often causes students to "sit" in the *demi-plié* or collapse in it when coming down. From this, progress to giving an *échappé relevé* (from 1st to 2nd positions) on the fourth count of *relevé,* then *relevés* continue in 2nd position 4x more and the student pulls into 1st position *demi-plié* (holding it briefly) on the "and" after the eighth count.

- After students have mastered the above with ease, add *relevés* on one foot: do above for 2 sets, but remain in 2nd *en relevé* after the second *échappé; demi-plié* in 2nd (*temps lié*) and *relevé* in *coupé (cou-de-pied) derrière* onto R. leg, and do 3 more *relevés* on R., then *temps lié* to L. support leg and repeat on L., then do 2 relevés on R., 2 on L. and then one each on R.,L.,R.,L. Close in 1st position at end. Keep same "syncopated" rhythm so emphasis is UP and HOLD. Make sure *demi-plié* is with heels firmly on floor.

- *Relevés* (spring) from two feet to one foot. Facing barre, *tendu* to 2nd, *demi-plié* in 5th front, *relevé* sharply and HOLD to *retiré devant (pirouette* position of working leg), close in 5th. Repeat until all students can lift hands off barre while in *retiré* and maintain balance for a few seconds. This later serves as good prep. for *pirouettes* exercise.

- Transfer of weight through the toes. Having students execute a *tendu devant*, then roll up to and through 4th position on half-pointe, and roll down into *tendu derrière* (with inside leg extended)—no

demi-plié—and back to *tendu devant*
second and to back. (Essentially, a *temp*
to do continuously, i.e., without stoppin
the 4th position, but rather moving
through the rolling-up and rolling-down position. Teaches students to roll down through the foot "in pieces." Emphasizes lifting up while rolling down (with the body) and shifting weight from one foot to the other easily.

- *Piqué.* Facing barre, students learn to do *piqué* to side (*de côté*) by stepping up to straight support leg (knee pulled up before *piqué)*, bringing working leg to *coupé* (or *retiré derrière* position). I usually begin this by teaching *dégagé* to 2nd in *fondu* (low leg), so that they push off standing leg in order to do *piqué.* Again, syncopate musically so that the student steps up quickly, then HOLD the *piqué* long enough for student to feel they are fully over the support leg and could balance there, then teach "replacing" one foot with the other—bring *retiré* foot down through 5th (*sous-sus*) while releasing support leg without bending it into *dégagé* 2nd *fondu* again in readiness for next *piqué*. The important things to stress here are: step onto straight leg, find "balance point" at top of *piqué*, and replace through 5th without bending *dégagé* leg. Push off each one from a good *fondu* position. Do not allow students to twist the body towards the "stepping" leg. Later do across floor, slow enough to make students find balance each time at top of movement, making sure they are stepping to 2nd and not turning the body towards the direction they are traveling.

Piqué done at barre before center ▲

- *Bourrées.* Facing barre and also across the floor in center, in soft shoes. Stress bending both knees while holding the ankle in position (not rolling over the arches). They should master this and be able to keep legs “crossed” and propel from the back foot rather than stepping out onto the front foot to initiate the movement so they are accustomed to working on high 3/4 pointe with bent knees.

BARRE Sample Lesson Plan: Pre-Pointe Class

NOTE: Emphasize exercises that use the foot and ankle for articulation and strength repeatedly. Depending upon length of your class time, use all or part of these exercises, or elaborate upon some to include longer combinations. Use Gail Grant, *Technical Manual and Dictionary of Classical Ballet* as reference for terminology. Ballet terms are in italics. “2x” means execute that movement two times, etc.

These exercises are meant to be done in soft ballet shoes, however they would be equally suitable as part of a beginning level pointe class for students already on pointe, done on pointe shoes. See next chapter, Beginning Pointe, for adaptations/variations of some of these exercises done *en pointe*.

1. ***Pliés*** (music suggested: slow 3/4), facing barre or one hand on barre
   a. *Demi-plié* in 1st position, straighten 1x
   b. *Élevé (*rise on straight legs to balls of feet) in 1st and lower heels with straight legs 1x
   c. Repeat (a) and (b)
   d. *Grand plié* in 1st and recover 1x
   e. *Port de bras (cambré)* forward only and recover 1x, *tendu à la seconde* and place working foot in 2nd position 1x
   f. Repeat (a) through (e), ending in 5th position, R. foot front
   g. Repeat (a) through (e), but with *cambré* back instead of forward, and *tendu devant* to place working foot in 4th position 1x
   h. Repeat (a). through (e) in 4th position with *cambré* back, then close into 5th position to end set

NOTE: Notice that *demi-plié* is always followed here by *élevé*. This encourages students to pull up the knees after each *plié.* Doing two *demi-pliés* in succession means this may not automatically occur.

2. ***Battement tendues* from 1st position** (music slow 4/4 or 3/4)
   a. *Battement tendu devant* from 1st position, then flex ONLY the metatarsals (toes) and come to pointed toe again 1x
   b. Now flex at the ankle and include toes (full foot flex), and come to pointed toe again 1x
   c. Roll through working foot to place it in flat 4th position on the floor 1x, then point again
   d. Close in 1st position; repeat *en croix.*

3. ***Battements tendues* from 5th position** (music: moderate speed 4/4 or 3/4), L. hand on barre, using R. leg. (Of course repeat all to L. side after, with R. hand on barre).
   a. *Battement tendu devant,* close (with straight legs) to 5th 1x
   b. *Battement tendu devant,* then rise onto both legs (transfer weight forward so that student is standing in 4th position on half-pointe on both feet); "roll" back down onto R. standing leg to *tendu devant* until "flat" on standing leg again with working leg in *tendu,*,
   c. Close in 5th position with *demi-plié* and straighten knees, 1x
   d. *Battement tendu à la seconde,* rise onto half-pointe in 2nd position, roll down on outside leg (moving away from barre, essentially a *temps lié* with straight legs) into *battement tendu à la seconde* with inside leg; now reverse movement and roll back onto inside (closest to the barre) leg, finishing in *battement tendu à la seconde* with R.
   e. Close R. leg into 5th position *devant* with *demi-plié.*
   f. *Battement tendu à la seconde* again with R.
   g. Close R. leg into 5th position *derrière* with *demi-plié*.
   h. Repeat all from (a) starting with R. leg *battement tendu derrière*.

4. ***Battement dégagé* and *battement piqué*** from 5th position, ("peppy" 4/4 music)
   a. *Battement dégagé devant* 3x ("even" accent, meaning one count to extend leg, one count to

close in 5th) on third one, do *battement piqué* 2x, close 5th.

b. Repeat (a) to side *(à la seconde)* and back (*derrière*), close 5th behind.
c. *Battement en clôche* (swing leg through 1st position, starting with *b. dégagé* to back on count "1" then take leg to front, back, front...
d. *Battement piqué en croix* starting front, without closing after each one, i.e., touch toe front, side, back.
e. Close 5th *derrière* and start all from (a) to back.

5. ***Pas de cheval, enveloppé*** from 5th position. (music 3/4 moderate tempo)
   a. Do *pas de cheval* (45⁰ in height) 2x *devant*, then 1x *enveloppé*, then one more *pas de cheval.* Do all (a) *en croix*.
   b. Pick up the front foot (R.) by bending the working knee slightly to *cou-de-pied*, close in 5th position *derrière.* Repeat, closing in 5th *devant*. Repeat closing in 5th *derrière*, then *demi-plié*.
   c. Repeat all from (a) starting to back.

6. ***Assemblé soutenu*** to half-pointe (3/4 or 4/4 moderate tempo)
   a. In 5th position, one hand on barre, R. front, slide front toe out into *tendu devant* and simultaneously bend supporting leg (*fondu*).
   b. Sharply pull working leg back to 5th position.
   c. Repeat (a) through (b) *en croix*
   d. Now repeat (a) to front, but when executing (b), pull working leg in to *sous-sus*
   e. Come down to floor with heels and *demi-plié* in 5th position.
   f. Repeat (d) through (e) *en croix*

7. ***Battement relevé*** and calf stretch (moderate 4/4)
    a. *Battement tendu devant* from 5th position, "roll through" foot into 4th position flat with both legs straight (this is a *battement relevé*, not to be confused with the term *relevé).*
    b. Press against floor slightly to release foot back to *tendu* position, close in 5th position without *plié*
    c. Repeat all *en croix.*
    d. *Battement tendu à la seconde*, alternating closing front and back in 5th 4x
    e. *Battement tendu à la seconde* a fifth time, this time lower foot to flat second position onto the floor, then flex foot <u>with heel remaining on floor</u> and both legs straight (calf stretch)
    f. Lower foot to flat 2nd position on floor
    g. Return to *tendu* position (point) and close 5th position with a *demi-plié*

8. ***Rond de jambe à terre*** (slow or moderate 3/4) from standard preparation, 1st position
    a. *Rond de jambe à terre* in 6 counts (half-time) *en dehors à terre* 4x
    b. *Chassé en avant* (forward) passing through 1st position into 4th position
    c. *Relevé* in 4th position, take arm *en haut*
    d. *Demi-plié* in 4th position, *relevé* again in 4th position
    e. *Pivot* towards barre (half-turn without coming down) to face opposite direction at barre (change barre hands)
    f. Reverse the *pivot* to face initial position again
    g. *Demi-plié* again in 4th position and *temps lié* (transfer weight to back leg) and end in *battement tendu devant* with L. front

h. Repeat from (a) *en dedans* (*pivot* turn away from barre)
i. End with balance by drawing *tendu* foot into *sous-sus*, arms *en haut*

9. ***Battement frappé*** (quick 2/4 or 4/4), start facing barre in 5th position, R. front, standard preparation of *battement tendu à la seconde* to *sur le cou-de-pied devant* with R.
   a. Using Cecchetti form of this exercise (i.e., from a *cou-de-pied* with ball of the working foot slightly flexed but not pressing into the floor): do *battements frappes* 7x *à la seconde*, alternating *cou-de-pied* placement as back, front, etc.
   b. The 8th *battement frappé* becomes a *jeté* (jumped), landing on R. foot in *fondu* with L. up in back in *cou-de-pied*
   c. *Relevés* (from a *fondu* each time) on R. foot with L. up in back in *cou-de-pied* 2x
   d. *Pas de bourrée dessous* (under) traveling to R., ending with L. front in 5th position
   e. Preparation with L. leg, standard preparation of *battement tendu à la seconde* to *sur le cou-de-pied devant* with L.
   f. Repeat all starting with L. from (a) through (e)

10. ***Battement fondu*** (slow 3/4), one hand on barre, begin R. foot front in 5th position
   a. Pick up working foot to mid-calf on straight supporting leg
   b. *Fondu* on standing leg
   c. Straighten standing leg while holding working leg at mid-calf *devan*t
   d. *Fondu* again on working leg, then extend working leg *devant* as standing leg straightens

e. Bring working leg back through 5th position as a *tombé* onto working leg (in *fondu*) and lift back leg to mid-calf simultaneously
f. *Piqué* onto straight back leg while bringing R. leg to *retiré devant*, hold briefly, close to 5th *derrière*—now L. foot is in front
g. Repeat (a) through (f) to back, *piqué* over (*dessus*) to finish with R. front again
h. Battement *fondu à la seconde* 2x
i. Close working leg to *sous-sus* with R. front
j. *Soutenu* (half turn) to L. side and repeat (a) through (i) on opposite side

11. ***Petits battements sur le cou-de-pied*** with "spring" (Cecchetti) ***relevés*** (quick 2/4 or 4/4), start in 5th position with R. front, facing barre, no preparation
   a. Quick *demi-plié* in 5th on "and" before first count of the music
   b. *Sous-sus* on count "1" and <u>hold</u> for counts "2-3-4"
   c. Repeat from (a)
   d. *Échappé relevé* to second position and hold as before, do 2x (*changé)*
   e. Pick up back foot to *cou-de-pied* on "and"
   f. *Pas de bourrée dessous* (travels to R.) to end with L. foot front 5th
   g. Do *tendu à la seconde* preparation to *cou-de-pied devant* (for *petit battement*)
   h. Do *petits battements* with R. for remaining 4 counts, end with R. foot closing in 5th *derrière.*
   i. Repeat all with L. front 5th to start

12. ***Rond de jambe en l'air*** and ***grand battement*** (strong march 4/4) start one hand on barre, 5th position, R. front
   a. *Grands battements* 2x *devant*

b. *Grand battement à la seconde and rond de jambe en l'air* (singles) 2x, close 5th position, R. foot *derrière*
c. *Grands battements* 4x *à la seconde*, alternating closing front, back, front back
d. Repeat all from (a) starting to back
e. When students are ready, do this exercise entirely *en relevé*, only coming down when closing *derrière* as in (b)

13. ***Bourrée* at barre** (2/4 or 4/4, moderate tempo)
    a. Facing barre, holding with two hands, students do *demi-plié* and *relevé* (*sous-sus*)
    b. Students then pick up front foot, then back foot to low *cou-de-pied*, lifting a slightly bent knee, at slow (half-time) tempo, one foot at a time, on slightly bent knees
    c. Students gradually increase speed until *bourrée* is done as fast as they can do correctly
    d. Students then travel slightly down barre in direction of front foot, turn away from barre in direction of front foot and make a small circle, returning to place at barre
    e. Students change feet during bourrée after they return to barre, lower to demi-plié to finish in 5th position flat
    f. Students repeat all with opposite foot front, travel to opposite direction, etc.

14. **Stretch** (optional and if time permits) do any form of stretch that incorporates the "runner's stretch" facing barre, wherein feet are parallel to start, then one foot reaches backward, flat on floor, front leg bent, pelvis kept facing front and pushing forward with weight kept on front foot as much as possible. Sitting floor stretches also recommended.

Runner's Stretch: L. correct hip position, R. is incorrect

CAUTION: Never allow students to sit on the floor and literally "sit" on each other's pointed toes or arches, nor should teachers or students press down hard on the pointed toes/arches manually. This is dangerous and not only painful, but could cause young underdeveloped bones to break or fail to form properly. Likewise, devices sold in which the foot is inserted and forced into an arch are equally dangerous, or at the least, a waste of money. The best way to improve the arch is simply to use the foot correctly and exercise often with tendues, etc. Flexion and pointing are excellent. Never try to force the arch artificially. The same danger applies to standing barefoot or in soft shoes upon the toes. Clutching the toes under to achieve this "trick" involves using the foot entirely incorrectly for ballet technique.

<u>CENTER Lesson Plan: Pre-Pointe Class</u>

1. ***Épaulement,* with *tendu & dégagé*** (4/4, moderate tempo)

a. Beginning in 5th position, R. front, facing corner 2: *Battement tendu devant* 4x
b. *Battement tendu derrière* with L. leg 4x
c. *Glissade* with R. en avant towards corner 2, opening arms to second
d. *Glissade* again with R. en avant, now stepping up (small *développé devant* with R.) to *sous-sus* towards corner 2, taking arms to 5th *en haut*
e. *Demi-plié* in 5th and repeat *sous-sus*
f. *Détourné* (rotate towards back foot, feet change place) ending in 5th with L. front and end facing corner 1
g. Reverse combination from (a), meaning, begin with *battement tendu derrière* with R. 4x, then do *battement tendu devant* with L. 4x, and do *glissades* traveling backward (*en arrière*)
h. Optionally, instead of (g), simply repeat from (a) starting with L. foot exactly the same as with (a) through (f)
i. Optionally, repeat entire exercise with *dégagés* instead of *tendues.*

2. ***Adagio tempo* exercise** (slow 3/4) Begin R. foot front in 5th position, facing 5 (front)
   a. *Demi-plié* in 5th and straighten
   b. *Fondu* on L. standing leg while picking up R. leg into *cou-de-pied devant*, straighten standing leg
   c. *Fondu* again on L, while extending R. leg to 45° *devant en relevé*, <u>hold one count</u>
   d. Close to *sous-sus* with R. front
   e. Do (a) through (d) *en croix*

3. ***Relevés* with *sautés*** (quick 2/4 or 4/4)
   a. Begin in 1st position, facing 5 (front), *demi-plié* on "and" before first count of music

b. *Sauté* in 1st position 2x
c. *Relevé* in 1st position (sustained), then *demi-plié* in 1st
d. *Échappé sauté* from 1st to 2nd position
e. *Sauté* in 2nd position
f. *Relevé* in 2nd position (sustained), then *demi-plié* in 2nd
g. *Relevé* onto R. leg only, taking L. leg to *cou-de-pied derrière*
h. *Demi-plié* in 2nd position again
i. *Relevé* onto L. leg only, taking R. leg to *cou-de-pied derrière*
j. *Demi-plié* in 2nd position
k. *Sautés* 3x in 2nd position
l. On last count, jump back into 1st position

4. ***Petit allegro*** (quick 2/4 or 4/4) Begin 5th position, L. foot front, facing front (corner 5)
   a. *Glissade sans changé* (quick, no change) to R.
   b. *Jeté dessus* (over) with R. as landing leg
   c. *Relevé* on R. with L. leg held off floor, *derrière*, 2x
   d. *Fondu* on R. with L. leg held off floor, *derrière*
   e. *Pas de bourrée dessous* (travels to R.), quick, ends with L. front
   f. *Changement*
   g. *Pas de chat* traveling L., hold landing in 5th position one count, 2x
   h. *Dégagé à la seconde* in *fondu* with L. as preparation for…
   i. *Soutenu* turn to R. shoulder, ends with R. front
   j. *Changements* 2x
   k. Repeat from (a) to other side

5. ***Piqué*** practice center floor (moderate 3/4 or mazurka 6/8) start R. foot front 5th position *croisé,* facing corner 2
   a. *Glissade* to half-toe (small *developpé devant* with R., then push off back leg and step up to *sous-sus,* ends R. foot front *croisé*), taking arms *en haut*
   b. Lower heels to *demi-plié* 5th position
   c. Change body direction to face 5 (audience, front) and repeat (a) *à la seconde*, changing feet when closing in *sous-sus*
   d. Lower heels to *demi-plié* 5th position, L. foot is front
   e. Change body direction to face corner 1 and repeat (a) *en arrière* (backwards), without changing feet when closing in *sous-sus*
   f. Lower heels to *demi-plié* 5th position
   g. *Chassé en avant croisé* towards corner 1, ends in *tendu derrière* with R. foot behind
   h. *Fondu* on standing leg and bring working leg, R., into *cou-de-pied derrière* at same time
   i. *Piqué* onto straight R. leg while bringing L. leg to *retiré devant, tombé* to (h) position
   j. Repeat (i), end in *tombé* again
   k. *Pas de bourrée piqué dessous* (travels to L.)
   l. *Battement tendu à la seconde* with L., close to L. foot front 5th position
   m. Repeat from (a) to other side

6. ***Piqué arabesque positions, traveling*** (moderate 3/4 or 4/4) From upstage L. corner of studio : begin in 5th position, R. front, effacé
   a. With small *developpé devant* with R. as preparation on "and", *piqué* in 1st *arabesque* towards downstage stage R. corner on first

count, taking arms through first and opening to *arabesque* position

b. *Tombé* forward until L. leg into "lunge"

c. Repeat (a) but instead of *tombé,* roll down through supporting leg and foot (straight leg) while holding working leg in *arabesque*

d. *Balancé* backward (*en arrière*) stepping onto L.

e. Step forward onto R. and *soutenu* turn to R. shoulder, ends with R. foot front

f. Repeat across floor traveling on the diagonal

g. Optional: repeat this exercise by doing (a) in 2nd arabesque and 3rd arabesque (Cecchetti)

7. ***Bourrées*** traveling ("running" continuous music similar to *petit battement*, or use adagio)
    a. Students begin in two columns, one on stage R. and one on stage L. and *bourrée* towards center of room
    b. Students cross lines, remembering the usual rule: stage L. dancer crosses in front of stage R.
    c. After reaching other side of room, each student does *bourrées* in small circle around self, and changes front foot
    d. Students do (a) again, now returning to original places.
    e. Alternately, this can be done in a circle traveling clockwise and counterclockwise, or changing arm positions every 4 counts, etc.

Chapter Four

The Beginning Pointe Class

Your students have now been prepared for pointe work by a year or more of pre-pointe class and both you and the dancers are looking forward to their first actual year on pointe. Be sure to stress to them that in this first year, especially the first semester, they will be facing the barre for pointe almost entirely until they gain the strength to dance in the center on pointe.

You may be combining a technique class for an hour-and-a-half with a final added half-hour for this basic barre work. Ideally, if they have an hour devoted to pointe entirely, it will be preceded by a technique class as a warm-up. It is not a good scenario to schedule a pointe class directly after a jazz or other dance class. If that is done, a proper ballet warm-up should be included in the pointe class, preferably (in the case of a beginning level class) one in soft ballet shoes.

At beginning stage, I like to do a one-hour technique ballet (off pointe) class followed immediately by a half-hour of pointe, spent entirely at the barre, mostly facing the barre. They should be doing at least three to six ballet technique classes per week at this stage, with one or two of them including this level of pointe work. Toward the <u>end of the first year</u>, students may do some two-footed *relevés* in center, i.e., *sous-sus, échappé relevé, assemblé soutenu, glissade to pointe.* If you accompany your beginning pointe classes as a group to buy and fit their first pair of shoes, remember that each student will need shoes suited to the physiology of their foot (strong shank on a weaker foot or heavier child, longer vamp on a high arch, etc.) The fit should be snug without "growing room."

Teaching goals for beginning pointe should include:

- Students should be able to roll up and roll down off pointe and achieve a good position at the top of the *relevé*, "pulling up out of the shoe" without sickling, pronating, clutching toes, rolling over, or overusing the barre, and with knees pulled up and body placement maintained. Students should be able to maintain turnout when rising and return to turned- out position when lowering heels to the floor .

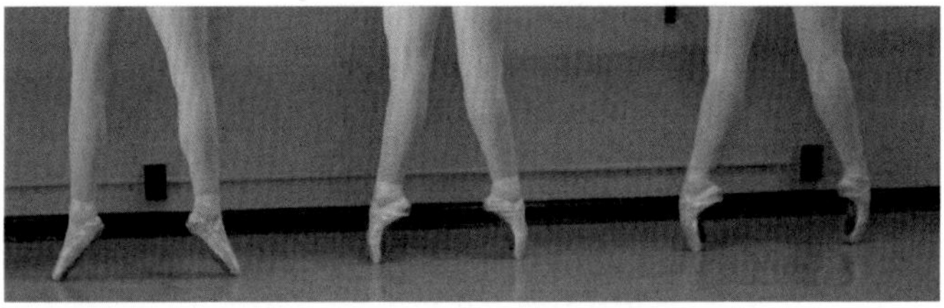

▲In above photo, far left, feet not able to achieve full pointe; center, correct with weight lifted up and out of shoes; far right, rolling over too far with weight downward into shoe.

- Students should be able to spring up to pointe by using the *demi-plié* correctly, in all positions, without undue stress or overuse of the barre, and be able to hold the *relevé* position with knees lifted and body weight distributed forward slightly over the toes. In the case of weaker students, in my experience, it is better to have them more forward than backward in their placement, since that will at least cause them to use the back and inside leg muscles; eventually, when strength is gained, the student will be able to straighten more in upper body. Leaning back causes overdevelopment of derrière and thighs, encourages bent knees, and puts undue stress on the spine.

The Basics of Pointe

In order to achieve a full pointe position, the dancer must either:

- Rise to pointe with legs straight (*elevé*)
- Rise to pointe with a preparatory *demi-plié* (spring) or *relevé*
- *Piqué* (step up to pointe)
- *Piqué "jeté"* (jump slightly onto full pointe, as with quick *piqué tours* in succession

Likewise there are several methods for descending from a full pointe position to "flat" with the heels on the floor:

- Rolling down through the shoe, passing through 3/4 and 1/2 pointe to either straight legs or *demi-plié*
- Springing down with a slight jumping movement into either *demi-plié* or straight legs
- *Tombé* (stepping/falling) down onto one or both legs
- *Coupé* (quick replacement of one foot by the other foot

Each of these movements should be incorporated into your pointe classes. Special attention should be paid to the descent from pointe so that it is smooth, lacking undue impact on the legs, and preferably almost silent.

TWO LESSON PLANS FOR BEGINNING POINTE CLASSES:

BARRE I: Sample Lesson Plan for Beginning Pointe Class (for a half-hour done on pointe immediately following a regular hour or hour-and-a-half ballet technique class) Lesson Plan II is designed for a full hour pointe class or second semester work.

A. ***Slow élevés with demi-plié*** in 1st, 2nd and 5th positions (music: slow 3/4 or 4/4, adagio tempo. NOTE: If using 3/4 tempo, the exercise below refers to 1 count meaning "1-2-3").
   a. Facing barre in 1st position, rise slowly in 4 counts with straight legs, being sure to roll through the high 3/4 position before coming to full pointe position.
   b. Roll down in 4 counts to flat 1st position, keeping knees straight
   c. Rise slowly as in (a) in 2 counts
   d. Lower to 3/4 pointe, keeping heels high off floor, in 1 count
   e. Rise again to full pointe in 1 count
   f. Lower to flat first position, straight knees, 2 counts
   g. *Demi-plié* in 1st and *battement tendu à la seconde.*
   h. Repeat this from (a) to (g) in second position, *battement tendu* and close in 5th position with R. foot front.
   i. Repeat this from (a) to (g) in 5th position, *battement tendu* with L. and close in 5th with L. foot front.
   j. Repeat this from (a) to (g) in 5th position with L. front, *battement tendu à la seconde* and return to 1st position at end of exercise.

B. ***Battements tendues* from 5th position** (music: moderate speed 4/4 or 3/4), L. hand on barre, using R. leg. (Of course repeat all to L. side after, with R. hand on barre). This is the same exercise as (3.) for pre-pointe barre, but now all half-pointe transfers of weight are onto full pointe. Suggest teaching this first facing barre, later do one hand on barre.

a. *Battement tendu devant,* close (with straight legs) to 5th 1x
b. *Battement tendu devant,* then rise onto both legs (transfer weight forward so that student is standing in 4th position onto full pointe on both feet); "roll" back down onto R. standing leg to *tendu devant* until "flat" on standing leg again with working leg in *tendu,*,
c. Close in 5th position with *demi-plié* and straighten knees, 1x
d. *Battement tendu à la seconde,* rise onto full pointe in 2nd position, roll down on outside leg (moving away from barre, essentially a *temps lié* with straight legs) into *battement tendu à la seconde* with inside leg; now reverse movement and roll back onto inside (closest to the barre) leg, finishing in *battement tendu à la seconde* with R.
e. Close R. leg into 5th position *devant* with *demi-plié.*
f. *Battement tendu à la seconde* again with R.
g. Close R. leg into 5th position *derrière* with *demi-plié*.
h. Repeat all from (a) starting with R. leg *battement tendu derrière*.

C. ***Battement dégagé and battement piqué en croix***. Suggest teaching this first facing barre, later do one hand on barre.

a. *Dégagé devant* with R., close 5th front (even accent musically, i.e., one count to *dégagé* and 1 count to close)

b. *Dégagé* again *devant*, close in 5th with *demi-plié*
c. *Dégagé* again *devant* and *battement piqué* 2x, close 5th
d. Repeat from (a) *à la seconde* and *derrière*
e. From 5th with R. foot *derrière,* lift working foot to *cou-de-pied derrière* and place it in 5th with R. foot *devant*
f. Repeat (e), ends with R. foot in 5th *derrière*
g. Repeat all from (a) starting to back

D. ***Assemblé soutenu*** to full pointe (3/4 or 4/4 moderate tempo) This is the same exercise as (6.) for pre-pointe barre, but now all half-pointe transfers of weight are onto full pointe. Suggest teaching this first facing barre, later do one hand on barre.

a. In 5th position, one hand on barre, R. front, slide front toe out into *tendu devant* and simultaneously bend supporting leg (*fondu*).
b. Sharply pull working leg back to 5th position, flat, both legs straight.
c. Repeat (a) through (b) *en croix*
d. Now repeat (a) to front, but when executing (b), pull working leg in to *sous-sus*
e. Come down to floor with heels and *demi-plié* in 5th position.
f. Repeat (d) through (e) *en croix*

 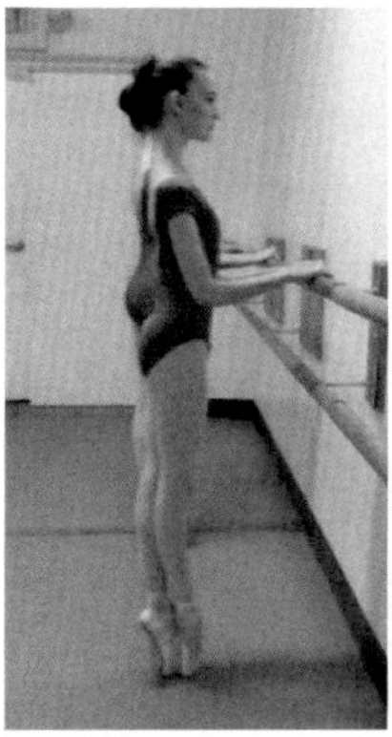

Assemblé soutenu, pulling working foot back toward standing leg and into *sous-sus* from a *dégagé* of *développé* preparation ▲

E. *Cecchetti ("spring") relevés on two feet* Sharp music accent, 2/4 or 4/4. Teach facing barre.

a. In 5th position, R. front, *demi-plié*
b. *Sous-sus*, pulling legs together—do not over cross 5th *en relevé*!
c. Repeat (a) and (b)
d. *Échappé relevé* to second position
e. *Demi-plié* in second position (flat)
f. Pull legs together into *sous-sus*, now with L. foot front in 5th.
g. Repeat (alternates feet)

F. *Coupé, piqué* practice at barre Sharp musical accent, 2/4 or 4/4. Teach facing barre.

a. With R. foot front, 5th position, lift L. foot *derrière* sharply while doing *fondu* (bending) the standing R. leg, musically do this on "and" before first count.
b. Step up (*coupé, piqué*) onto L. leg and bring R. working leg to *retiré devant* simultaneously
c. *Tombé* (come down) onto R. foot, flat

d. Repeat (a) and (b), do 4x total
e. At end of fourth *piqué*, close *en pointe* in *sous-sus* with R. foot front
f. Now *tombé* onto R. foot and lift L. into *cou-de-pied derrière*
g. *Pas de bourrée dessous* (under) en pointe, traveling to R. with feet changing, end in *demi-plié* 5th position with L. front, flat.
h. *Sous-sus (relevé)* 1x, *demi-plié*
i. Repeat (a) through (h) now with L. foot starting in front ▼

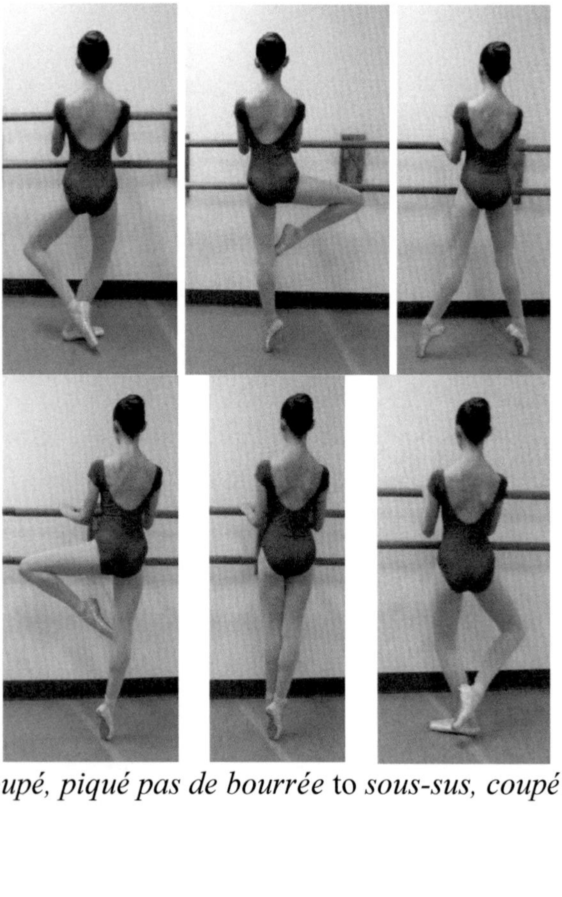

Coupé, piqué pas de bourrée to *sous-sus, coupé* ▲

G. ***Bourrée at barre*** (2/4 or 4/4, moderate tempo) Same as pre-pointe exercise, but now on full pointe.

a. Facing barre, holding with two hands, students do *demi-plié* and *relevé* (*sous-sus*)
b. Students then pick up front foot, then back foot to low *cou-de-pied*, lifting a slightly bent knee, at slow (half-time) tempo, one foot at a time, on slightly bent knees
c. Students gradually increase speed until *bourrée* is done as fast as they can do correctly
d. Students then travel slightly down barre in direction of front foot, turn away from barre in direction of front foot and make a small circle, returning to place at barre
e. Students change feet during *bourrée* after they return to barre, lower to *demi-plié* to finish in 5th position flat
f. Students repeat all with opposite foot front, travel to opposite direction, etc.

H. **Cecchetti *("spring") relevés* from two feet to one foot** (often called *sissonne simple*), facing barre

a. Begins 5th position, R. foot front, *demi-plié* in 5th on "and" in music before first count
b. *Relevé* from both feet and lift front foot to *cou-de-pied devant*
c. *Demi-plié* in 5th again on two feet
d. Repeat but now lift back foot to *cou-de-pied derrière*
e. Repeat (a) through (d) 4x total
f. After fourth *relevé*, do not close 5th, but roll down through support leg into *fondu* (bent

leg) while holding working leg in *cou-de-pied derrière*

g. Pas de bourréé dessous to 5th position in *demi-plié* with L. front (travel to R.)
h. *Sous-sus* with L. front
i. *Demi-plié* in 5th
j. Repeat all with L. foot starting front

I. ***Glissade*** (stepping up) ***to pointe*** Similar to *piqué* insofar that it refers to stepping onto a straight leg, although the preparation for the step may be a small *développé* or a *dégagé* in the direction of the step with working leg while doing a *fondu* with standing leg). Suggest teaching first at barre *à la seconde* only, with *dégagé* rather than *developpé* to encourage stepping onto straight supporting leg. Use a march or similar strong music 4/4, moderate tempo.

a. Facing barre, begin R. foot front in 5th position: *dégagé* sharply *à la seconde* with R. while doing *fondu* (bending) supporting L. leg
b. Step up to 5th position *en pointe*, bringing L. leg *derrière* in 5th
c. Come down to *fondu* again on L. leg and *dégagé* as before with R.
d. Repeat (a) through (c) traveling to R. down the barre
e. On fifth repeat, close L. leg *devant* instead in the 5th position (*glissade changé*)
f. *Soutenu*, full turn away from barre, to R. shoulder, feet changing places in 5th
g. End in *demi-plié* 5th position, again facing barre, with R. foot front
h. Repeat to same side. Then change and do all starting with L. foot front and traveling to L.

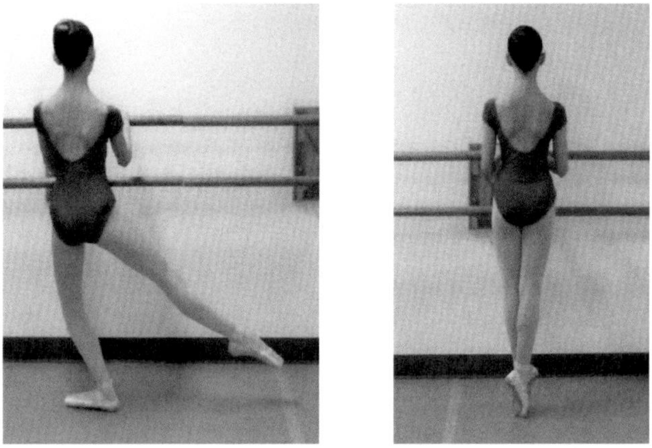

Glissade to pointe at barre, traveling & stepping up to R.

<u>CENTER I Lesson Plan: Beginning Pointe Class</u>

At end of the year, if students are sufficiently strong, *sous-sus* and *échappé relevé* may be done in center in very short combinations. I usually put off *piqué* steps in center because students will often try to bend the knees when stepping up without barre support. *Glissade* to pointe done *en croix* may be possible, but first-year students cannot be expected to correctly execute *bourrées* across the floor yet, or (in many cases) *passés relevés*. They will have time to master these later. In a half-hour class, time will be spent almost entirely at barre.

NOTE: Students who are unable to find a secure and correct position of the foot while *en pointe* after the first year should repeat that year. Going forward with bad habits or physical problems does not solve the problems, but rather makes them more noticeable and more difficult to correct when more advanced steps are approached. Some students and certain kinds of foot structures are simply not suited to pointe work; encouraging them to continue will only result in a depressed and unhappy student. Such students should be mentored towards other dance forms where pointe work is not necessary.

It is the teacher's responsibility to check the position of the foot INSIDE the pointe shoe to be sure students are not clutching toes, curling toes (sometimes the smaller toes will automatically curl when pointing, however), dancing on their knuckles, or "grabbing" the ankle in order to *relevé* as opposed to stretching the foot properly and lifting up and out of the shoe when *en pointe*. It's beneficial to have a demonstration of these when students first acquire their shoes, or even before they go for a first-shoe fitting. These photos demonstrate possibiities you will see among your students.

RIGHT we see "clutched toes" & arch, often resulting from tight ankles or flat arches. Avoid this very incorrect development of the foot! Teachers should correct this early on in training by looking at the student's foot barefoot.▶

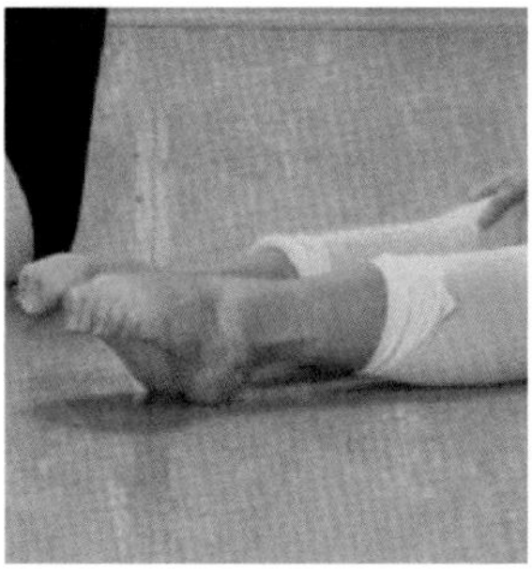

RIGHT: Extending arch to use toes this much weakens the foot especially for pointe, and may result in dancing "on the knuckles" on pointe.▶

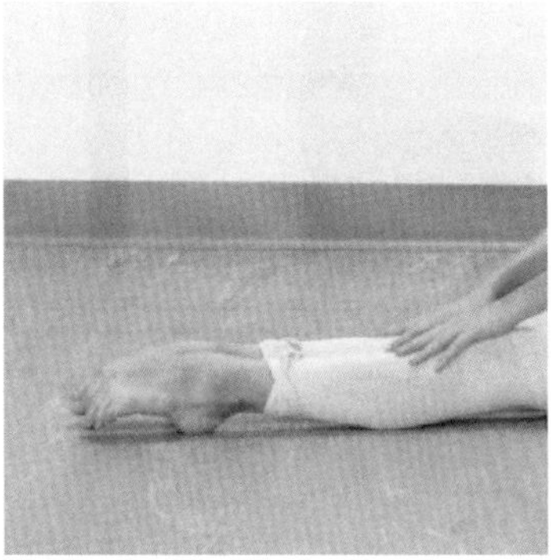

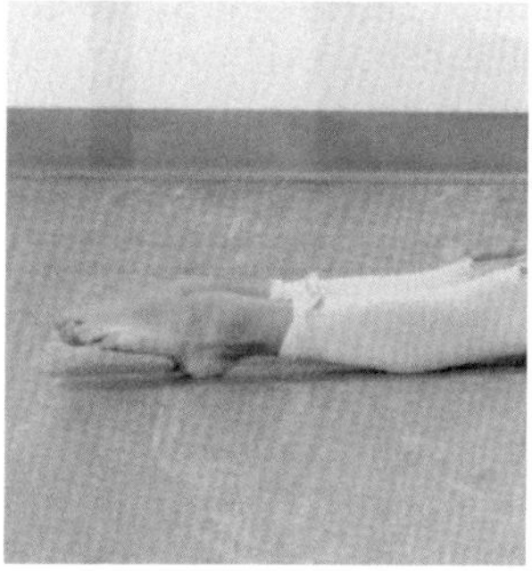

LEFT: Same feet, now with arch well-used and with toes "reaching" outward, very necessary for strength & correct position on pointe

◄

<u>BARRE II: Sample Lesson Plan for Beginning Pointe Class</u> (for a full hour done on pointe after a regular hour or hour-and-a-half ballet technique class) If this class is not preceded by a warm-up given in a regular ballet technique class, it is important to give a more comprehensive barre.

A. ***Demi-plié, grand plié, cambré*** (slow 3/4 tempo)
   a. Facing barre, do 2x *demi-plié* and *elevé* in 1st position
   b. Repeat 1x more, now adding a *demi-plié* while on pointe (be careful not to roll over the feet, but rather hold the ankles in starting position during *plié*) and straighten
   c. Balance briefly in 1st *en pointe* with arms in 1st (front), roll down from *elevé*, then *tendu à la seconde* and place foot in 2nd position
   d. In 2nd position do *grand plié* and straighten
   e. *Cambré* forward (*port de bras*) and recover
   f. Repeat *grand plié* in 2nd position
   g. *Battement tendu à la seconde*, flex foot and point again, close front in 5th position
   h. In 5th position, repeat (a) through (c) now balancing in *sous-sus* and ending with *tendu devant* and place foot in 4th position

i. In 4th position repeat (a) through (c) and end with balance in 4th and *tendu devant* then close to 5th at end.

B. Then repeat this exercise from Lesson Plan I: ***Slow elevés with demi-plié*** in 1st, 2nd and 5th positions (music: slow 3/4 or 4/4, adagio tempo. NOTE: If using 3/4 tempo, the exercise below refers to 1 count meaning "1-2-3").

1-4 a. Facing barre in 1st position, rise slowly in 4 counts with straight legs, being sure to roll through the high 3/4 position before coming to full pointe position.

5-8 b. Roll down in 4 counts to flat 1st position, keeping knees straight

1 2 c. Rise slowly as in (a) in 2 counts

3 d. Lower to 3/4 pointe, keeping heels high off floor, in 1 count

4 e. Rise again to full pointe in 1 count

5 f. Lower to flat first position, straight knees, 1 count

6 7 8 g. *Demi-plié* in 1st and *battement tendu à la seconde.*

h. Repeat this from (a) to (g) in second position, *battement tendu* and close in 5th position with R. foot front.

i. Repeat this from (a) to (g) in 5th position, *battement tendu* with L. and close in 5th with L. foot front.

j. Repeat this from (a) to (g) in 5th position with L. front, *battement tendu à la seconde* and return to 1st position at end of exercise.

C. ***Battements tendues* from 5th position** (music: moderate speed 4/4 or 3/4), L. hand on barre, using R. leg. (Of course repeat all to L. side after, with R. hand on barre). Suggest teaching this first facing barre, later do one hand on barre.

a. *Battements tendues devant,* close (with straight legs) to 5th 4x
b. Small low *développé devant,* then step forward onto full pointe into 5th as *sous-sus* on both feet.
c. Close in 5th position with *demi-plié* and straighten knees, 1x
d. Repeat (a) through (c) *à la seconde*
e. *Sous-sus* 2x, coming down each time in *demi-plié* 5th
f. Repeat (a) through (c) *derrière*
g. Repeat (e) *à la seconde*
h. *Battement tendu à la seconde* again with R.

D. ***Battement dégagé and battement piqué en croix***. Suggest using one hand on barre.

a. *Dégagé devant* with R., close 5th front (accent "in", 5th position closing on each beat of music). No *demi-plié*.
b. *Dégagé* again *devant*, *battement piqué* 2x, close in 5th position in *demi-plié*. Hold 1 ct.
c. Repeat from (a) *à la seconde* and *derrière*
d. Repeat entire set, starting again *devant*.

E. ***Cecchetti ("spring") relevés on two feet*** Sharp music accent, 2/4 or 4/4. Do facing barre.

a. In 5th position, R. front, *demi-plié* on "and"
b. *Échappés* 2x *à la seconde, changé*
c. *Échappé* 1x, and *demi-plié* in 2nd position flat
d. *Sous-sus*, pulling legs together—do not over cross 5th *en relevé*! End L. foot front, 5th in *demi-plié* 5th.

e. Repeat (a) through (d) starting with L. front and ending the set with R. front again
f. Do 4 complete sets

F. ***Coupé, ballonnée piqué*** practice at barre Sharp musical accent, 2/4 or 4/4. Teach facing barre.
a. With R. foot front, 5th position, lift L. foot *derrière* sharply while doing *fondu* (bending) the standing R. leg, musically do this on "and" before first count.
b. Step up (*coupé, piqué*) onto L. leg and bring R. working leg to *dégagé à la seconde* simultaneously
c. *Fondu* (bend) standing foot, and come down flat while simultaneously bending the working leg at the knee to end in *cou-de-pied derrière* (*Ballonnée piqué*)
d. Repeat (a) through (c) by stepping up *piqué* onto R. (opposite leg)
e. At end of second *ballonnée piqué*, *pas de bourrée dessous* (travels to R., ends with L. foot front in 5th)
f. Do 2x *changements* (jumped), hold 1 count
g. Repeat all starting with L. foot front.

G. **Cecchetti *("spring") relevés* from two feet to one foot (*retiré relevé* and *passé relevé*)** facing barre
a. Begins 5th position, R. foot front, *demi-plié* in 5th on "and" in music before first count
b. *Relevé* from both feet and lift front foot to *retiré devant*
c. *Demi-plié* in 5th again on two feet
d. Repeat but now lift back foot to *retiré derrière,* close 5th again on two feet

e. Repeat (a) but *passé relevé* and close 5th *derrière*
f. Repeat (d) but *passé relevé* and close 5th *devant*
g. With R. foot in 5th *devant, battement tendu à la seconde,* hold 1 ct.
h. Close into 5th front, in *demi-plié*
i. On next *relevé* to *retiré devant*, execute a one-quarter turn to R. *en dehors*, to one hand on the barre, holding working leg up in position, and taking R. arm to *pirouette* position in front.
j. On next *relevé* to *retiré devant*, execute a three-quarter turn to R. *en dehors*, to end facing barre, close R. leg derrière.
k. Repeat to opposite side.

H. Repeat **Exercise (G)** from Beginning Barre I sequence.

CENTER II Lesson Plan: Beginning Pointe Class

1. ***Glissade*** (stepping up) ***to pointe*** Similar to *piqué* insofar that it refers to stepping onto a straight leg, although the preparation for the step may be a small *developpé* or a *dégagé* in the direction of the step with working leg while doing a *fondu* with standing leg). Suggest teaching first *à la seconde* only, with *dégagé* rather than *developpé* to encourage stepping onto straight supporting leg. Use a march or similar strong music 4/4, moderate tempo. Do *en avant*, change feet when closing and doing *à la seconde*, stress stepping onto already-straight leg and pulling second leg "under you" when closing in *sous-sus*—especially when stepping *en arriére.* Will repeat in

a pattern of a square. Then reverse and start with L. front. Arms optional.

2. ***Assemblé soutenu*** to full pointe (3/4 or 4/4 moderate tempo). Do this in center starting with R. foot *derrière* in 5th and take working leg *à la seconde* alternating legs, traveling forward 8x. Then repeat traveling backward (*dessous, en arrière)* 8x.

3. ***Relevés in center on two feet.*** Suggested sequence: Do *sous-sus* 3x, then 1x *échappé changé*. Do four to eight sets total.

4. **Walks *en pointe*.** Across floor, as a prelude to doing traveling *bourrées*, have students do three steps forward *en pointe*, come down on third one and brush opposite leg *devant* as a *dégagé*. Similar to a character dance polonaise step. Alternates legs.

5. ***Assemblé soutenu*** traveling, across the floor, stepping up to pointe and finishing in *demi-plié* after each step up to sous-sus.

6. ***Soutenu turns***, one turn at a time, across floor, stepping up to pointe, and closing each turn in 5th in *demi-plié*.

Chapter Five

The Intermediate Pointe Class

NOTE: By this stage students should be enrolled in a separate pointe class (preferably two) weekly as well as three to five ballet technique classes per week. They should be able to wear their shoes for the entire pointe class (usually one hour in duration).

1. *Teaching goals*:

- The emphasis now is on developing strength. The student should be able to execute steps in center floor in simple combinations with balance and control, done at moderate tempi.

- Students should (by end of year) be able to combine pointe steps with simple jumps and connecting steps in center or at barre without difficulty.

- Students should be able to execute multiple *relevés* from two feet to one foot (i.e., *passé relevé*) and from open positions (i.e., from 4th position *demi-plié* to *retiré devant*, like *pirouette* prep.)

- Students should be able to do some multiple *relevés* on same foot in succession, and should be learning to pull supporting toe under for such *relevés*.

- Student should be able to sustain balance on one pointe in center, i.e., *piqué arabesque*.

- Student should be able to do steps without tension in arms, neck, head, or upper body.

2. *Sample exercises*:

- Barre work should now include some exercises with *demi-plié en pointe*, holding ankles (not rolling over arches) as preparation for jumps en pointe, *relevés* from two feet to one foot (*passés relevés*) and *relevés* on one foot, i.e., successive *ballonnés relevés,*

- Barre exercises should be lengthened and involve different movements to develop speed and stamina.

- Center work should include what has been done previously at barre, with particular emphasis on using the *demi-plié* correctly and being able to sustain a *relevé* position. This includes *échappés* to 2nd and 4th, *assemblé soutenu, glissade* to pointe, etc.

- Center work should use traveling steps such as *bourrée* and *piqué* done *en diagonale*. Use moderate tempo to encourage finding balance at top of each *piqué*. Progress to *piqué* single turns *en dedans*.

- Center work should include practice of *passés relevés* from 5th, both with alternating legs and with same leg, traveling back and forward. Then *passés relevés* doing quarter turns, also from 5th, as prep. for *pirouettes*.

- I find it helpful at this stage to do walks and runs in pointe shoes (both on and off pointe) as they will do on the stage in choreography, which is an often neglected practice. They can also do these in center (walks) if strong enough, without emphasis on speed, but rather on precision and clarity.

LESSON PLAN FOR INTERMEDIATE POINTE CLASS:

BARRE EXERCISES: Lesson Plan, Intermediate Pointe Class for a full hour-long class on pointe preferably held directly after a one or one-and-a-half hour ballet technique class. Half of pointe class time (or more) should now be spent in center work.

1) ***Demi-* and *grand pliés***, one hand on barre, slow 3/4
   a) *Demi-plié* and straighten in 1st position
   b) *Battement tendu à la seconde* and close back to 1st position
   c) Repeat a) and b), but do not close in 1st ; hold tendu position 1 ct.
   d) Press over the working toe by bending working leg (lunge outward from barre slightly) to stretch the arch of working foot, keeping hips level
   e) Return to *tendu à la seconde* position (point, both legs straight)
   f) Flex working foot at ankle with straight legs
   g) Repeat d)
   h) Repeat e)
   i) Place working leg in 2nd position flat
   j) *Grand plié* in 2nd position 2x
   k) *Battement tendu à la seconde* with outside leg and port de bras towards (over) the barre, using outside arm
   l) Close to 5th position with outside leg devant
   m) *Port de bras* away from barre in 5th position flat
   n) In 5th position repeat a)
   o) Repeat b) but with *battement tendu devant*
   p) Repeat n) and o); hold *tendu devant* 1 ct.

q) Repeat d) through i) all to front, end by placing working foot in 4th position flat
r) *Grand plié* in 4th position 2x
s) *Port de bras* forward and *cambré* back
t) End by closing to 5th position, *sous-sus* and brief balance with arms en haut

2) ***Battements tendues* and *relevés***, moderate 4/4
a) Battement tendu devant 4x, quick tempo
b) *Demi-plié* and rise to *sous-sus* and hold
c) Battement tendu devant 4x *en pointe* without coming down (close to sous-sus each time)
d) Roll down into *demi-plié* 5th position
e) *Échappé relevé* to 4th position
f) Return to 5th position *demi-plié*, straighten
g) Repeat a) through f) to side (with *échappé* side *changé)*, and to back do 4th *échappé* as before
h) Finish set with *battement tendu à la seconde* 8x, ending with R. front in 5th
i) *Assemblé soutenu devant*, pulling up to *sous-sus* and *soutenu* to face other side
j) Repeat all on opposite side

3) ***Pas de cheval, assemblé soutenu (coupé) piqué***, moderate 3/4 or 4/4 (4/4 will be quicker version)
a) In 5th flat, one hand on barre, do *pas de cheval* to 45° height devant
b) Repeat a) but end in *fondu* on standing leg and working toe *à terre* (on the floor)
c) Assemblé soutenu (pull working leg into *sous-sus)*
d) Drop to flat on front foot, ending with back foot up in *cou-de-pied derrière (coupé)*
e) *Piqué* onto back foot and bring working leg to *retiré devant*
f) Close to 5th flat in slight *demi-plié*

g) Repeats *en croix*; note that to side feet change, i.e., *sous-sus derrière* and drop down on back foot, *cou-de-pied* is with front foot, *piqué* to *retiré derrière* (toe behind knee), etc.

4) ***Échappé relevé changé*** with transfer of weight
   a) Facing barre, R. foot front in 5th, do *échappé relevé* into second position
   b) *Demi-plié* in second position, flat (do not close the *échappé)*
   c) *Relevé* from two feet onto one foot, picking up L. and placing it in *retiré devant*, i.e., *temps lié* with *relevé*
   d) Close 5th position, L foot front
   e) Repeat a) through d) with transfer of weight onto opposite leg

5) ***Sauté and relevé* combined** (4/4 or 2/4, quick)
   a) Facing barre, *sautés* 2x in 1st position, ending in *demi-plié* 1st
   b) *Relevé* (spring) in 1st position 1x, end in *demi-plié* 1st
   c) *Échappé sauté* into 2nd position *demi-plié*
   d) *Sauté* again in 2nd position
   e) Repeat *relevé* as in b) but in 2nd position, end in *demi-plié* in 2nd
   f) Do *relevés* 3x more in 2nd position
   g) At end of 3rd *relevé,* come down to *demi-plié* in 2nd position flat and *temps lié* (transfer weight to R. leg and *tendu à la seconde* with L.) and close into 1st flat
   h) Repeat all, doing *temps lié* at end to opposite direction

6) ***Piqué* and multiple *relevés* on one foot** in succession (4/4 or 2/4)

a) Facing barre, *piqué* down barre, traveling, on R. 3x; *relevé* after third *piqué* on same leg
b) Repeat this exercise but do a) 2x and do 2 *relevés* on same leg
c) Elaborate on this exercise by making the simple *relevés* (in *cou-de-pied derriére*), into *ballonnées relevés*, alternating *cou-de-pied devant* and *derriére* on b)
d) Increase difficulty by doing with one hand on barre and do *piqués* forward *(en avant)*

7) ***Pirouette* preparation** at barre (moderate ¾)
   a) Repeat Exercise G for Beginning Pointe Barre II, g) through k) only
   b) Add: *battement tendu à la seconde* (facing barre, as k) ends, with front foot
   c) Close *demi-plié* 5th front and hold
   d) Do full *pirouette en dehors* from 5th, end with working leg still up in *retiré devant*, remain on pointe
   e) *Développé à la seconde* with working leg and close 5th position *derrière*
   f) Repeat all to L. side
   g) Note: *développé* may also be done to *arabesque* before closing 5th. This is good practice later for partnering work.

8) ***Sissonne* at barre (*de côté*) traveling side** (facing barre)
   a) Repeat *sissonne simple* Exercise H. from Beginning Pointe, Barre I, a. through e.
   b) Then add: *sissonne de côté* (to side) *dessus changé,* i.e., travel slightly to R. on spring *relevé* to *dégagé à la seconde* with L. as working leg and <u>hold one count</u>, then close

working leg in front 5th, flat, in *demi-plié* with L. foot front

c) Repeat b) to L. side, close R. front
d) Repeat b) and c)
e) Repeat all reversed, using *sissonne de côte dessous* (under), traveling in direction of back foot and closing working leg in 5th flat in *demi-plié* behind.

9) ***Échappé relevé changé à la seconde***, changing musical accents (fast 2/4 or 4/4)
   a) Facing barre do *échappés relevés changés* 2x, with even accent (*échappé* on ct. 1, close on ct. 2)
   b) Then do *échappés relevés changés* 4x, with accent "in" on 5th positions each count (i.e., twice as fast)

<u>CENTER EXERCISES for Intermediate Pointe</u> (order of exercises is optional) I suggest simple combinations for intermediate pointe, emphasizing only 2-3 different movements so that students may concentrate on the "how" and not the "what-comes-next" aspect of performing them.

10) ***Assemblé soutenu* and *walks on pointe en avant* and *en arrière*** (moderate 4/4)
   a) Starting in 5th position, R. foot behind, do *assemblé soutenu dessus* (over, back foot extends *à la seconde* and closes front) with R.
   b) Repeat with L.
   c) Walks forward (*en avant*) *en pointe* 4x, taking care to cross but not overcross in *sous-sus* each step; legs open slightly to side each time, then cross into 5th (*sous-sus*)
   d) Repeat a) through c), ends with L. front
   e) *Tombé* (roll down through foot) onto front foot and pick up back foot to *cou-de-pied (coupé)*

f) *Pas de bourrée dessous* (travels L.), ends R. front
g) *Changements (sautés)* 3x, ends L. front
h) Repeat entire combination traveling *en arrière* (backward), i.e., do *assemblé soutenu dessous* (front foot finishes behind), walks backward, *pas de bourrée dessus* (over)

11) ***Glissade en pointe* using *épaulement* positions and varied *port de bras*** (moderate 3/4 or 4/4)
a) Starting in 5th position facing corner 2 (Cecchetti), in *croisé devant* with R. front, *glissade en avant (en pointe* to *sous-sus)*, using correct *croisé* arm position, roll down to 5th position flat.
b) Repeat a)
c) *Échappé* to 4th position *croisé*, close 5th
d) *Échappé changé* to 2nd position, changing to *en face* (wall 5), close 5th
e) *Échappé* to 4th position *croisé,* now to corner 1, L. front, hold (do not close)
f) *Demi-plié* in 4th position flat
g) Transfer weight as *temps lié* to *tendu croisé derrière*, close 5th position *croisé* to corner 1
h) Repeat all on left side.
i) To increase difficulty, give single *pirouette en dehors* from *demi-plié* in 4th with *sous-sus* afterward. NOTE: do this after pirouette practice has been given from 5th and at barre.

12) ***Piqués traveling* and *turning en dedans*** 3/4 or 4/4
a) Across the floor diagonally, students do single *piqué* (no turn) 3x in succession with working foot coming to *retiré derrière*, traveling, keeping arms in 3rd position (Cecchetti)—keep arms still during this movement

b) On fourth *piqué,* turn *en dedans* and close arms to 1st position (French, Russian—called 5th position in Cecchetti)
c) Progress this combination by decreasing number of simple *piqués* and increasing turns—i.e., do 2 *piqués* and 2 *piqués tours en dedans*

NOTE: Stress keeping R. arm in front throughout when traveling to R. side, and not opening both arms in order to turn. For a single or even double *piqué turn en dedans*, it is only necessary to close the second (back) arm into 1st position. Otherwise students become dependent upon opening the first arm to obtain force for the turn which is not only unnecessary, but also a technical flaw. Students should be stepping to side for each turn, and not turning the body to face the direction of the turn.

13) ***Piqué arabesque, tombé***, traveling, mod. 3/4 or 4/4
a) Traveling on the diagonal, do small *développé effacé devant* with R. arms in front, step up (*piqué*) to *arabesque* (open to 1st *arabesque* arms)
b) *Tombé (failli)* through to fall forward upon L. leg into small "lunge" with R. leg behind and R. leg straight, arms coming to 1st position (front); now both feet are flat, L. arm comes front
c) Repeat a) and b)
d) To elaborate on this exercise, give "running" *glissade* before each *developpé* (*glissade precipitée)* done on "and" before first count of music
e) As students progress they should strive to hold a brief balance in each *arabesque* position

14) ***Pirouettes* in center from 5th, *en dehors,*** mod. 3/4
   a) Starting 5th position, R. front, do *passés relevés* 2x with R., closing back, then front
   b) *Battement tendu à la seconde* with R., close in 5th front in *demi-plié*
   c) *Pirouette en dehors* from 5th, full turn, and close behind
   d) *Sous-sus*, arms en haut
   e) Repeat a) through d) to opposite side with L. leg

NOTE: Teaching pirouettes from 5th before 4th en dehors discourages students from twisting the hips towards the back foot in the 4th position preparation. Later, as this becomes a good habit the students will do 4th position preparations without "cheating" the hips. Exercise may be done initially as 1/4 then 1/2 turns *en dehors.*

15) ***Chainé tours*** across floor on the diagonal, use 2/4 or fast coda
   a) Before these, be sure to practice *soutenu* turns singly across the floor (see CENTER II, exercise number 6, for Beginning Pointe)
   b) Begin by having students turn for 6 counts, then finish in 5th position flat, *demi-plié* for 2 counts
   c) Gradually increase turns, i.e., do *chainé tours* for 14 counts, then finish in *demi-plié* as in b)

16) ***Bourrées*** across floor traveling, mod. "running" 4/4 or 3/4 or adagio tempo music
   a) Begin by having student do *bourrées* on the diagonal across the floor, making sure they begin in "B+" with L. behind (when traveling to R.), and that they are using the back foot to

propel and initiate the step, rather than stepping out to the side with the front foot

b) Allow *bourrèes* for 14 slow counts, then give a "rest" measure of counts where they can come down off pointe

c) Gradually increase counts the students can maintain full pointe until they can cross entire studio floor

17) ***Piqué tours en dehors*, preparatory exercise** traveling on the diagonal across floor, 3/4 mod. tempo

a) Traveling on the diagonal across the floor, students begin in upstage corner R., with R. foot front in 5th position, *effacé*; *tombé* onto R. (small lunge) with weight transferred onto R. in *fondu* and L. leg extended straight behind, flat. R. arm is in front (first) and L. arm in second position

b) Slight *rond de jambe en l'air* (very low) with L. leg *en dedans*

c) *Piqué* onto L. by bringing L. foot through sous-sus position in front of R., both legs now straight as student steps up

d) Simultaneously, R. leg lifts to *retiré devant* position and arms close into first position

e) Repeat a) through d) across floor

f) Gradually introduce the single turn *en dehors* with arms closing on the turn and opening to arm position used in a) on the *tombé* each time; emphasize spotting

NOTE: Students will tend to make this into a *soutenu* turn and lift working leg at the last possible moment—be sure come down on back (L.)t is a true *piqué* movement with one leg replacing another. Coordinating arms with legs is very important.

18) **Walks on pointe**, traveling on the diagonal as a prelude to doing polka step fully on pointe, give this version: use moderate 4/4
   a) Student starts in 5th position R. foot front, *effacé*
   b) Step up and forward onto R. (like a *glissade* on pointe), then…
   c) Bring L. foot behind to *sous-sus* position
   d) Come down back (L.) foot and using small *développé* to….
   e) Step up again forward onto R.
   f) Roll down on R. to flat in *fondu* while doing simultaneous small *développé devant* with L.
   g) Repeat a) through d) now using alternate foot

19) **Runs on pointe** traveling on the diagonal, use quick coda or other 2/4 music
   a) Student starts in *tendu devant effacé* in upstage corner 3 (Cecchetti) with R.
   b) Small runs on pointe with emphasis on keeping feet close together in 1st position or parallel, knees slightly bent
   c) Encourage students to eventually change arms as they run, i.e., first do with arms in *demi-seconde* position across floor, then do while arms progress through other positions including *arabesque* arms
   d) Practice running on pointe and then coming to half-pointe runs and vice versa so they can make easy transitions from one to the other as is often called for in choreography
   e) Practice doing runs that culminate in a *piqué arabesque* or other "still" balanced position

20) Combining ***petit allegro*** jumps with pointe steps, done as a center combination, moderate to quick 2/4 or 4/4

a) Start in 5th position facing wall 5, R. foot *devant*
b) *Changements* 3x, end with R. foot behind
c) *Glissade sans changé* to R.
d) *Pas de chat* to R., end with back foot up in *cou-de-pied*
e) *Pas de bourréé en pointe dessous*, ends with R. front (travels to L.)
f) *Sous-sus*
g) *Échappés changé* (to second) 4x *relevés, en pointe*
h) *Détourné* (turn as *relevé* towards back foot), end in *demi-plié,* ends with L. foot front
i) *Sous-sus*
j) Repeat all to L. side

Chapter Six

The Advanced Pointe Class

Students should now be enrolled in daily classes for technique with separate hour-long pointe classes, and/or be encouraged to wear pointe shoes for technique classes as well. I personally believe that an hour-and-a-half exclusively pointe class may be too long, especially if students have already had a typical hour-and-a-half technique class in the same day or immediately prior. Wearing pointe shoes throughout a two-hour rehearsal, for example, is not as demanding as an overly-long pointe technique class.

1. *Teaching goals*:

- Emphasis now is on building speed, clarity (technical precision), and stamina.

- Students should be able to combine steps and perform extended combinations or entire variations en pointe.

- Students should be able to do quick shifts of weight, multiple *relevés* on one foot, fast turns and other steps *en diagonale* and *en manège*, and jump well (landing softly) in pointe shoes. They should also be able to run (on and off pointe) easily, quietly and gracefully across the studio or stage.

- Students should be able to do a full technique class wearing pointe shoes, and be able to execute adagio steps as well as *petit allegro*, *batterie,* and *grand allegro* in pointe shoes with ease.

- It is often beneficial in a pointe class, to combine *relevés* with all jumps, or *piqué* with t*ombé*; in this way students learn to do all manner of steps in their pointe shoes, not just 'on pointe' steps. *Pirouettes* might easily be included in a jump combination, or adagio, alternating quick movements with slow ones, for example. This is how choreography for the stage often works, so it is excellent practice.

2. *Suggestions for steps to include in advanced level pointe classes* (Note: there are many other possiblities. These steps and others are part of the lesson plan barre and center exercises given in this chapter).

- At barre, *flic-flac en tournant, ballonnés relevés* and *ballonnés piqués, grand fouetté relevé* or *piqué*

- Jumps on two feet (*changements en pointe*), turns.

- In the center, students may execute multiple *pirouettes, fouetté* turns, *pas de cheval* and polka step en pointe, and jumps and/or hops on one pointe, or jumps landing on pointe.

- Students should be able to do extended *bourrées* across floor, and walks and runs en pointe.

- Hops on pointe on the same foot consecutively

- Consecutive *relevés* on one foot with the working leg held en l'air

BARRE Advanced Pointe Class Lesson Plan

I. ***Pliés*** (3/4, slow)
   A) Beginning one hand on barre, 1st position

B) *Demi-plié* in 1st and straighten
C) *Demi-plié, relevé* in 1st
D) *Demi-plié* on pointe, hold ankles in place, straighten, roll down to flat 1st
E) *Grand plié* in 1st, come up only to *demi-plié* position, then….
F) Descend again into *grand plié,* reversing arms, and finish on straight legs
G) Battement tendu à la seconde
H) Place R. foot in second position
I) In 2nd position do *demi-pliés* 2x
J) *Grand plié* 1x in 2nd position
K) *Port de bras* forward and *cambré derrière*
L) *Tendu à la seconde* and close in 5th position
M) Repeat A) through H) in 5th position, ending with *tendu devant* to 4th position
N) Repeat I) through K) in 4th position
O) End closing 5th position

II. ***Battement tendu*** from 5th position with ***ballonnée piqué*** and ***ballonnée relevé*** (4/4 or 3/4, moderate)

A) *Battement tendu devant* in 5th position, one hand on barre, accent "in" on the beat, 2x
B) Pas de cheval to *tendu à terre devant*
C) *Assemblé soutenu* (pull working leg into *sous-sus*)
D) *Coupé* (come down on front foot, pick up back foot to *cou-de-pied*)
E) *Piqué* onto back (inside) leg, lifting front foot *à la seconde* off floor at 45° (preparation for *ballonnée piqué*)
F) Sharply bring working leg to *cou-de-pied derrière* in *fondu*
G) Relevé while opening working leg back into 45° *à la seconde (ballonnée relevé)*
H) Sharply bring working leg to *cou-de-pied devant* in *fondu*

I) Without lowering working foot to floor, *relevé* into *retiré devant* from *cou-de-pied devant*
J) *Développé* coming to flat *fondu* (at full height) with working leg *devant*
K) *Piqué en avant* into *arabesque* onto working leg
L) *Fouetté* towards barre 1/2 turn into extended leg *devant*, facing other side
M) Close to 5th position, repeat all on L. side

NOTE: This exercise may also be done reversed, i.e., begin with working leg *derrière* so that *fouetté* is reversed (*piqué en arriére, fouetté* away from barre ½ turn into *arabesque* at end).

III. ***Battement dégagé*** from 1st and 5th position with quick ***échappés relevés changés*** (4/4, moderate)

A) Facing barre, do *battement dégagés* 4x *à la seconde* with R. leg, closing in 1st position, quickly
B) Repeat, closing 4x into 5th position (close back, front, back, front), close last one in *demi-plié*
C) *Échappés relevés changés* to 2nd position 4x with accent in (down) in 5th position each time, quickly
D) *Sissonne de côté* (to R., traveling) *ouverte*, ends with L. leg extended at 45° to side, held
E) *Fondu* on support leg
F) *Pas de bourrée* (*simple*, not *piqué*) *dessous*
G) Repeat with L. leg beginning *devant*

IV. ***Flic-flac en tournant* and *relevés* on same leg with working leg changing positions** (2/4 or 4/4, moderate)

A) Facing barre in 5th position, R. front, do *relevés* onto alternating feet, lifting working leg to *cou-de-pied devant*, (change legs, then…) *derrière, devant*, *derrière*, coming down into 5th position after each one

B) Do one additional lift *devant* and lower into *fondu* on supporting leg, R. leg up in *cou-de-pied devant*
C) *Fondu* on supporting leg while extending working leg *à là seconde* at 45° as preparation move
D) *Flic-flac en tournant en dedans*, ending *en pointe* with R. leg up in *cou-de-pied derrière*, hold briefly
E) *Relevé* on working leg once in *cou-de-pied*, then lift and *relevé* again in low *attitude derrière*, lift and *relevé* again in *arabesque*
F) *Fondu* in *arabesque*
G) Pull working leg into *sous-sus derrière*
H) *Demi-plié* in 5th position
I) Repeats to L. side
J) Repeat all reversed, thus *flic-flac* is *en dehors*
K) After D*) en dehors*, do successive *relevés* from *cou-de-pied devant* in *cou-de-pied*, then *retiré devant*, then (from *développé*) *à la seconde* at full height

V. ***Battement en clôche and grand fouetté relevé*** (3/4, brisk)

A) In 1st position, one hand on barre, do *battement en clôche*, as follows: brush R. leg front, back, front—finish in *fondu* on supporting leg, with working leg at full height *devant*
B) *Grand fouetté relevé* turning towards barre, leaving working leg up, ending in *arabesque* on pointe, facing other side
C) <u>Hold *arabesque* for 1 full count</u>
D) Repeat *clôche* with same working leg (flat on supporting leg) to front and back
E) *Grand* *fouetté relevé* away from barre leaving working leg up, ending in front extension at 90° (or better)

F) Repeat entire combination reversed, same leg, i.e. begin *clôche* by taking working leg back first—thus first *fouetté* will be away from barre and second one will be towards barre.

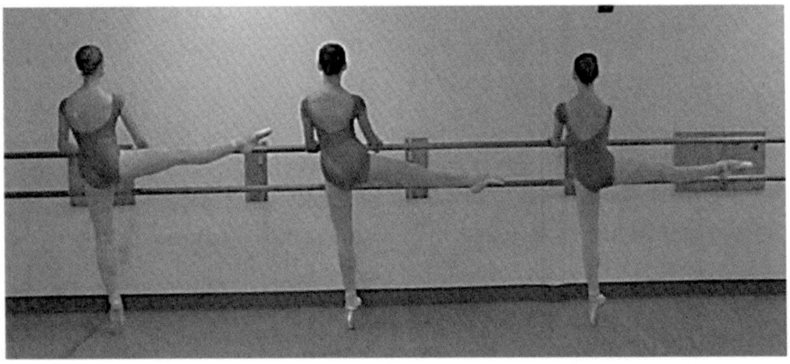

VI. ***Preparatory exercise for jumps on two feet on pointe*** (2/4 or 4/4)

A) Facing barre begin 5th position, R. front—*demi-plié* in 5th
B) *Sous-sus*
C) Repeat A) and B)
D) *Demi-plié* on pointe in 5th
E) *Changements* on pointe 2x, ends with R. front
F) Straighten legs and roll down into 5th flat
G) Repeat all starting with L. foot front

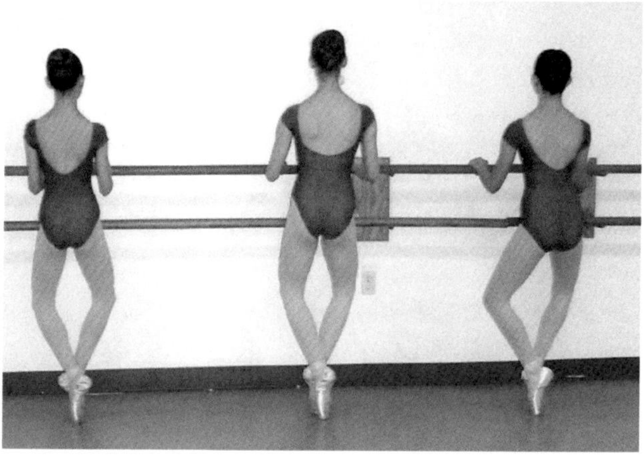

Note: Ankles are held so that the foot does not "roll over."

VII. ***Preparatory exercise for hops on one foot on pointe*** (2/4 or 4/4)

A) One hand on barre, 5th position with R. front, do polka step forward as: *glissade* on pointe (step up on R., bring L. foot to 5th behind, staying up)
B) Step forward again on R. and slight hop on R. as L. foot does small *développé* through to *devant*

C) Repeat with L. foot initiating the step, ends with R. foot 45° devant
D) Roll down to *fondu* (flat) on supporting leg
E) Step onto straight R. leg *en avant* into *arabesque*
F) *Fondu* slightly on R. leg while still on pointe and execute 2x *temps levé en pointe* (hops) on R. in *arabesque*
G) *Assemblé* (jump legs together) into 5th position in *demi-plié*

VIII. ***Ballonnées relevés c***onsecutively on same leg (3/4)

A) Begin one hand on barre, 5th position, R. foot front—on first count, *fondu* on standing L. leg and lift R. leg *to cou-de-pied devant*
B) *Ballonnées relevés sur place devant* 3x
C) *Coupé* (*tombé* onto R., lifting L. leg to *cou-de-pied derriére*
D) *Relevé* on R. leg, with L. leg in *retiré derrière*
E) *Coupé* again (*tombé* onto L., lifting R. leg to *cou-de-pied devant*)
F) Repeat B) but now travel forward slightly on each *relevé*
G) Repeat C) and D), but on D), turning towards barre on *relevé* 1/2 turn to end facing other side, bring *retiré derrière* to *retiré devant*
H) *Fondu* on L. leg dropping L. *retiré* into *cou-de-pied devant*
I) Repeat all now facing other side

CENTER EXERCISES for Advanced Pointe

IX. ***Développé*** **and** ***grand battement relevé en pointe*** **using body directions** (3/4, moderate)

A) Begin *croisé devant*, 5th position, R. foot front (facing corner 2)—do small step forward onto R.
B) Using slight *fondu* as preparation on standing leg, execute a *développé relevé* with L. leg to *écarté* body position (toe to corner 2), hold extended leg briefly up
C) *Tombé* slightly across body into *croisé* 4th position *demi-plié* onto L. leg, incline upper body to L.
D) Quick *coupé* and step forward *croisé* onto L. in 4th *demi-plié*
E) Repeat A) and B) and C) with R. leg, ending in 4th position *croisé* to corner 2
F) Repeat A), B) and C) now substituting *developpé piqué* instead of *developpé relevé* to *écarté* corners
G) Repeat A), B) and C) with *enveloppé relevé*
H) After final 4th position to corner 2 do *soutenu* turn to R. shoulder, arms *en haut,* ends L. foot front 5th position *demi-plié*
I) *Glissade* forward onto pointe and *bourréé en avant* 4 counts
J) Repeat all to L. (Suggestion: after *bourréé*, allow second class group to do R. side, then do all to L.)

X. ***Pirouettes en dehors* and *en dedans* in *attitude derrière* and *arabesque*** (3/4 moderate tempo)

A) Begin in "B+" with R. foot back, en face—*balancé de côté* to R. and L.
B) *Tombé* onto R., *pas de bourrée dessous* to R., ending in 5th position with L. front
C) Détourné sur place, ending in 5th position, R. front, *effacé*
D) Pas de basque towards corner 1, ending in "lunge" 4th, L. front, back leg straight behind, *croisé*
E) *Pirouette en dedans* in *attitude derrière*—arms join in front, then one or both arms come to *en haut*

during *relevé* so that they are in position by the time the turn occurs

F) Finish turn with leg up in *attitude croisé derrière*, in slight *fondu* on supporting leg
G) *Relevé développé* into *arabesque croisé derrière*
H) *Glissade en arrière* and *développé devant croisé* with L.
I) *Chassé en avant* (*croisé* to corner 1), finish in same lunge position as in D) above
J) *Pirouette* in *first arabesque* to L, end in *arabesque* facing wall 6
K) *Tombé (failli)* forward onto R. leg, ending in "B+" croisé, L. foot behind
L) Repeat on opposite side

XI. **Jumps on pointe, two feet** (2/4, 4/4, brisk)

A) Starting in 5th position, *en face*, with R. front
B) On count 1, *demi-plié* in 5th
C) *Échappé relevé* to 2nd position on count 2
D) Repeat B) and C) 3x more (4 *échappés* total), 8 cts.
E) *Demi-plié* in 5th with R. front (ct. 1)
F) *Sous-sus* (ct. 2)
G) *Demi-plié en pointe* (ct. 3)
H) *Changements en pointe* 3x
I) Roll through into 5th position flat, L. front, straighten legs (cts. 7-8)
J) Repeat with L. front to start

XII. ***Ballonnées relevés*** in center floor for stamina and strength (3/4 or 4/4 tempo—3/4 demands more control)

A) Begin in 5th position en face, R. foot front
B) *Ballonnées relevés devant sur place* (without traveling forward) with R. working leg 4x
C) Change feet (*coupé*) and do *ballonnées relevés derrière* with L. working leg 4x

D) Change feet (*coupé*) and *do ballonnées relevés à la seconde* 4x with R. working leg
E) *Tombé* onto R. leg (side) *and pas de bourrée dessous*, end in 5th position *demi-plié* with L. front
F) Repeat all starting with L. foot front

XIII. **Polka step on pointe, *en diagonale*** (2/4)

A) Start in B+ in upstage corner 3, R. foot behind
B) Using opposite arm front, other arm in second, step forward onto R. *en pointe (effacé)*
C) Without coming down, bring back foot into front foot into *sous-sus*
D) Step forward again onto R.
E) With slight hop *en pointe* on R., do small *developpé devant* simultaneously with L.
F) Repeat all with L. foot stepping forward, B) through E) using opposite arms as well
G) When students have mastered this traveling *en avant*, try *en arrière*
H) **Variation on this exercise**: after polka step to R. and L. once, add *pas de cheval en pointe* (hopping) 2x with R. and 2x with L.

XIV. ***Ballonnées relevé*s traveling *en avant en diagonale*** (3/4 or 4/4)

A) Start R. front 5th position, *effacé*, upstage corner 3
B) *Glissade en avant* onto pointe (ends *sous-sus*, R. front)
C) *Ballonnées relevés* 2x in succession
D) *Tombé* forward onto R. into low *arabesque*, L. behind, ending in slight *fondu*
E) *Pas de bourréé sans changé en avant en pointe*, end in 5th position flat, R. front
F) Repeat all across floor

G) As students master this, increase difficulty by doing *ballonnées relevés* 6x before *tombé*

XV. **Preparatory exercise for *fouetté tours* in center** (3/4, 4/4, march, etc.)

A) Begin R. foot front, 5th position, *demi-plié*
B) *Retiré relevé* lifting R. foot on count "1"
C) Return to *demi-plié* 5th position, R. front
D) *Pirouette en dehors* from 5th position, ending in 5th position with R. front
E) Repeat D) but end with small *developpé devant* with R. in fondu on supporting leg
F) *Fouetté turn* 1x to R. using appropriate arms to R.
G) Step forward onto R. as *glissade en pointe* into *sous-sus* with R. front, *demi-plié* in 5th R. front
H) To increase difficulty, after students have mastered single turns, do *fouetté turns* 4x before *glissade en avant*

XVI. ***Fouetté tours* traveling *en diagonale*** (2/4, coda, or quick 4/4)

A) Start upstage in corner 3, preparatory position as *tendu croisé devant* with L. front
B) *Piqué tours en dedans en diagonale* towards corner 2, twice, to R.
C) (*Coupé*) and *tombé* onto R. as preparation for…
D) *Piqué tour en dehors*, ending in *developpé devant* in *fondu* on L. supporting leg
E) *Fouetté tour en dehors* 1x
F) Repeat from A) across floor
G) Ultimately, try multiple *fouettés tours* across entire floor *en diagonale*
H) Some students may be able to do double *fouettés tours* interspersed with singles

XVII. **Multiple *relevés* on same foot on pointe, traveling** (4/4)

A) From downstage corner 1, traveling backwards (*en arrièrre*) towards upstage corner 3, begin with R. foot front in 5th position, facing corner 1
B) Do quick backward "scoots" on R. leg with L. leg held in *arabesque* 4x on the diagonal
C) Do *relevés* in *arabesque* 2x, traveling backward, keeping working leg up
D) Repeat across floor
E) To increase difficulty, do *arabesques relevés* 6x

XVIII. **Multiple *relevés* on same foot on pointe in center combination** (2/4, 4/4)

A) Begin R. foot front, 5th position *en face*
B) Step (*piqué*) *à la seconde* (towards wall 8) onto R. bringing L. leg to *attitude derrière*, L. arm up
C) *Relevé* in *attitude croisé derrière*
D) *Relevé* again, extending L. leg into *arabesque croisé* and changing to appropriate arms
E) Without dropping L. leg, *relevé* again doing *fouetté* to face corner 1 while taking working L. leg into *attitude croisé devant*
F) *Relevé* again, bringing L. into *retiré devant* and turning body slightly to face *en face*
G) *Demi-plié* in 5th position with L. front
H) *Pirouette en dehors* from 5th position to L., closing L. foot *derrière*
I) *Pas de basque en avant* to finish in *sous-sus* with L. foot front.
J) Repeat all to other side

XIX. ***Grand allegro* with pointe steps** (heavy 3/4)

A) Start downstage corner 2, in *epaulé tendu derriére* with R. foot behind, R. arm front in *arabesque* position
B) *Coupé* (changing feet: jump onto R. foot and *dégagé devant* quickly with L.) and *piqué* in first *arabesque* to corner 2 on L.
C) Turn body to face back corner 4 in two steps onto R. and L., turning to R. shoulder
D) Step onto R. and *grand fouetté relevé* into *arabesque croisé* ending in *arabesque fondu,* L. leg up, facing corner 2
E) *Piqué* first *arabesque en avant* onto L.
F) Take 2 steps as before in C) as preparation, third step into *grand jeté en tournant*, landing in *arabesque fondu* on L. standing leg, arms go to *en haut* and open to second position
G) *Relevé* in *arabesque*
H) Step back onto R. and *balancé en tournant* turning towards L. shoulder and ending facing back corner 4
I) Step forward onto L. towards corner 4 and *grand jeté* 2x landing on R. each time
J) *Soutenu* turn to R. shoulder ending *sous-sus en face* with R. front
K) *Chainé tours en diagonale* to R. towards corner 1
L) End in pose, *tendu derriére* first *arabesque à terre* on R. leg and hold briefly

Chapter Seven

Teaching & Coaching Classical Repertoire (Variations) and Other Choreography on Pointe

Up to this point, students have spent many hours in the classroom buidling their technique. Now, finally, they can be introduced to using that ability as a tool, a "means to an end," rather than the end itself.

Some dancers will welcome this and take it in stride, while others will persist in believing that the mere execution of the steps alone constitute an adequate performance. A new challenge to teachers is to make pupils aware of this next big leap in their learning curve.

Variations (solos and group dances) from classical ballets are excellent for building stamina, increasing clarity, developing speed, and adding nuances to performance quality. This is where students extend their dancing beyond physical technique and learning steps; now they should also be encouraged to use elements of artistry, including musicality, acting, mime, the interpretation of a character role, and historical style differences that exist in each dance epoch. When teaching classical variations, explain to your students how style differences can strongly affect the authenticity of a performance, and how these differences often depend upon the most subtle of arm, head, or body movements.

In a well-constructed repertoire/variations class, the teacher will challenge students to infuse their dancing with different emotions: shyness, strength of purpose, or resignation, for example. Dances excerpted from the story ballets are rife with teaching possibilities: Giselle is trusting and naive in the ballet by the same name, while her counterpart, Myrtha, is cold and merciless; in *Swan Lake*, Odette is tender and vulnerable, while Odile is conniving and sly. *Romeo and Juliet* offers similar challenges for the men: they may be asked to dance a variation for Romeo the lover, or Mercutio the playful sidekick, or Tybalt the domineering family patriarch. In doing so, they soon learn to use facial expression and mime as well as steps to develop a character.

Dramatic ballerinas and leading male character dancers are becoming less common in this age of purely technical concentration in many dance companies.Yet the use of role interpretation and mime continue to be a vital part of many audience-pleasing ballets. These classes are best taught by former professional dancers who have personal experience in interpreting different roles and dancing a variety of emotionally demanding parts.

For teachers, it is important to do some research prior to taking on this task. No one has danced each and every pivotal role in every major ballet, and even if they are teaching dances that they have performed and are familiar with, they should remember that each company director probably put his/her own "spin" on the version they learned. When teaching, it is important to remain objective. Study several interpretations, and try to find the most original version possible, one without elaborate additions or obvious deletions. Adapt that version to your students' abilities—this is quite acceptable, and even in professional ballet competitions, usually expected.

Even if a very young student has impressive technical skills, the emphasis here should be on giving them appropriate-level dances that teach performance quality and on making a "connection" with the audience. If they are expected to perform overly-complicated or very difficult feats of strength "for show" they will often miss the importance of artistry. This often happens when directors are too anxious to promote a student's chances of winning in a competition environment by relying too heavily on technique and ignoring the positive effect that a well-chosen style and careful interpretation has upon professional judges.

And here is an important note that hopefully all teachers will remember: when teaching variations in a group class situation: always include *all of the students* in that lesson. Even if you know that not all will be performing it, they are all interested in learning, and should have their chance to perform it, if only for their fellow students. You may ultimately be surprised by the better performer, who may not be the "technical whiz" of the class but who has the sensitivity to make the dance appealing to an audience! They will all be challenged and it will bring out the best in each of them.

Students being taught variations as a private lesson, in preparation for a performance or competition, should be given a different approach. For them, the teacher needs to focus on the particular aspects of their technique and/or artistry that need to be honed. It is the student's responsibity to learn the steps quickly and accurately and be able to perform them well, because a private lesson needs to go beyond the basics.

Common sense dictates that only students deemed otherwise technically and artistically prepared should be encouraged to attempt participation in a professional-level ballet competition, since the purpose here is still promoting a learning experience for the dancer. It is sometimes difficult to explain this to an ambitious parent or student, but advising them to perhaps wait another year in lieu of becoming overwhelmed by the task or the outcome, is a responsibility that all teachers eventually need to address.

Choosing an appropriate variation

Aside from age recommendations, assuming some younger students may not yet be on pointe, here are some considerations that often determine what is appropriate: tempo (speed); style (i.e., Romantic, Classical, Contemporary); length (usually shorter variations should be taught first, gradually increasing stamina by teaching longer pieces); and technical difficulty (if your students are not yet ready for multiple turns, for example, choose a variation that does not include these). It is much better to compliment the abilities of a student rather than have her/him struggle through a series of "tricks" they cannot yet manage to do with ease.

In a classroom situation you are free to choose variations you feel suit your students' abilities. Recommended variations for less experienced dancers you may want to consider include: *Sleeping Beauty* (fairies, Red Riding Hood, Blue Bird, with possible exception of Lilac Fairy); variations from *Coppélia* (Swanhilda Act. III Pas, or Doll Variation); *La Fille Mal Gardée; The Fairy Doll; Harliquinade.* For older, stronger students, choose from a larger selection. Keep in mind that if you plan to have students perform these publicly in a ticketed performance venue you should restrict your choices to older ballets that are considered to be "in the public domain." Otherwise you may be subject to music and/or choreographic royalty payments. For purely classroom purposes, you may make changes to the choreography to accommodate the students' abilities.

Teaching and Coaching for Competitions

If you are preparing students for a serious amd legitimate ballet competition, you must adhere to the listed variations assigned to that particular age group or division. Some competitions allow variations outside of the list by prior approval; in that case, it is usually the teacher's responsibility to obtain any necessary choreography or musical releases and pay any royalties. Time restrictions as to length of music are strictly observed. Minor adaptations to the choreography to accommodate student age or ability are sometimes acceptable; read the requirements carefully when applying.

It is best to choose from the list provided and tailor the choreography, if need be, to your own dancers. Many competition judges will tell you that they prefer to see some of the lesser-known works because they may be inundated yearly with Sugar Plum fairies or swans! While those may be on the list, aim for a more original approach if possible. And if virtuosity isn't the goal, concentrate on the subtle nuances of style and presentation instead, if these are your dancer's strong points.

Bear in mind, as we discuss competitions, that this refers to mostly-ballet competitions that focus primarily on giving well-trained non-professional students a chance to be seen by noted company directors seeking to recruit dancers for the future. The prizes here are rarely "trophies" given out to every participant, and the students seeking to enter must submit a video or audition in order to register. They accept only a limited number of qualified applicants per age division. Age 9 is usually the youngest age, while some may not allow students under 12. Students may be offered summer scholarships to major ballet schools as a final prize. These are ballet-oriented events with strict guidelines and structured rules and often include master classes with reknowned teachers.

Many dance schools take large groups and some solos to competitions whose only admittance requirement is payment of a registration fee, and whose lengthy performances include all dance idioms with widely variant ability levels. Often standards are quite low and their *primary interest is as a profit-making venture*—participating dance schools receive a financial "kickback" per the number of students they bring, plus perhaps free hotel stays and other "perks." They also make money off the costumes they re-sell to students, since the schools serve as retailers for the costume manufacturers. In other words, the main focus is profit. At such events you may hear both students and parents speak critically or disparagingly of other schools or dancers—this does not promote the kind of atmosphere that should prevail. Competitions should be about, and for, the dancers.

For a list of serious ballet/dance competitions, use the Internet to find those that have a long-established reputations and require certain variations to be performed. These are usually reliable and participation, while perhaps a complicated process, is valuable because it ensures exposure to a challenging and viable group of competitors. Look for competitions that require a photo, or video, or an audition, or series or elimination rounds as part of the application process. The more discriminating the guidelines, the more likely it is to be a worthwhile venture. There are usually eliminations after every round of solos or group pieces in each age division.

Here are a few possiblities:

- www.yagp.org (Youth America Grand Prix)

- www.rad.org.uk (Royal Academy of Dance)
- www.prixdelausanne.org (Prix de Lausanne)
- www.theamericandancecompetition.com
- www.usaibc.com (US International Ballet Competition, Jackson, Miss.)

Remember, also, that parents and teachers who accompany students to these pre-professional competitions may not be allowed to observe all events, such as master classes. Again, the focus is on the dancers.

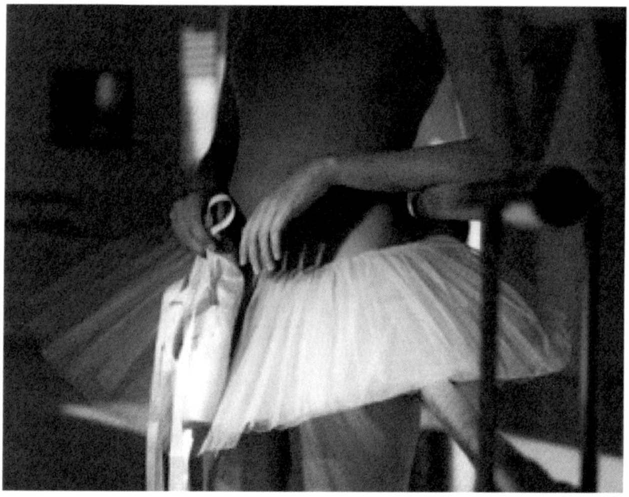

Chapter Eight

The Importance of Artistry

Dance is never a purely physical phenomenon. This becomes clear when witnessing a student, even one with extraordinary technical perfection, dance a particular solo and then seeing a seasoned professional perform the same role. All of the steps remain the same, the music is the same—why does one dancer stand out above another? What makes the interpretation of a role stay in the mind of the audience long after the performance has ended?

The answer to both questions has to do with skills that are often thought to be 'natural gifts,' or absorbed or developed intuitively. I call these *The Intangibles.* They are as important to a dancer as a well turned-out leg or a dazzling pirouette, yet they are often neglected by teachers. The assumption, perhaps by both teacher and student, is that these qualities are either inherently *there*, or that they cannot be taught. In this chapter that assumption will be challenged, since obviously some teachers are highly successful at turning out students who possess them, while others are not. I list these (with my own definitions) as:

1. *Musicality*—the ability to relate to, and be sensitive to, music, and to use musical accents and phrasing/attack.

2. *Acting*—being capable of creating a recognizable character from a dance role.

3. *Visualization*—using visual images or thoughts to enhance performance or to overcome stage fright or other negative mental 'blocks.'

4. *Memory retention* –the dancer's ability to remember corrections and apply them, and to learn choreography and retain long sections of movement.

5. *Imagination/creativity*—using imagery and original thought when teaching, choreographing dancing, or interpreting a role.

All of these 'intangibles' are in fact contributory to the overall perception of *artistry*. They distinguish the technically proficient dancer from the artist. Yet solid technical ability is also necessary before the dancer becomes a true artist. While some elements of *artistry* may be evident early on in training, they must go hand-in-hand with the mastery of physical skills so that the dancer is free to go *beyond* technique.

Musicality, in terms of teaching ballet, involves imparting both sensitivity (awareness) of music and its importance to the student, and the subtle nuances of accents and phrasing that enhance the dancer's performance. To this end, teachers should give combinations or steps to music of a suitable tempo and meter so that the class members can relate music directly to the step or combination. While a student is acquiring technique, it is equally important that he/she acquire respect for the music accompanying each exercise. Rhythm is inherent in most students because speech itself involves listening to cadences of sound.

This takes students to the next level of musical awareness: *accents and phrasing*. As students progress, they discover that to be an artist they must dance not just "to" the music, but dance the music itself. With that realization, musicality goes beyond 'keeping time' and the emerging artist learns to use it to highlight his performance. Both sensitivity and phrasing/accent awareness *can be taught* if the teacher gives it attention in class.

Once on the stage, the dancer may find that performing with technical expertise and musicality may not be enough; she must also use *acting ability* for *role interpretation* when necessary. And unlike a stage actor, the role must be conveyed to the audience through *pantomime and gesture* rather than words. Stage makeup and costuming may be helpful to define a character, but in some contemporary ballets these may only be suggestive rather than literal so it is up to the artist to find a way to make the audience believe she is someone else, and to express strong emotional reactions that may be essential to the story line. Even in non-story ballets, the performer must have a strong presentation on the stage. These qualities are best approached in specific classes geared to more accomplished students. Small dance studios without sufficient enrollment to justify such classes should therefore refer their upper-level students to attend dance schools that provide them, sometimes during summer intensives. In practicing actual roles, the dancers in these classes should learn to apply technique to expression.

Visualization, another 'intangible' idea, is tied to performing, and students can be taught to use it as a confidence-builder as well as an artistic tool. It is a highly personal concept. Young students are surprisingly susceptible and responsive to visualization. This is because they have active imaginations that function simultaneously with the realistic interpretations of what they see and hear around them. Teachers can use this to great advantage. The mere suggestion that they are 'leaves blowing in the wind' will evoke a mental picture they then *transform* into movement. For the older student who is more concentrated on technique, *visualization* can be used to create a *hyperawareness* of their surroundings. They can use it to create a 'virtual' stage set surrounding them, an elaborate unseen costume, or to *transform* an ordinary object into a stage prop. a "mental rehearsal" before an actual performance by visualizing a perfect rendition of steps, spacing, mime, musical phrasing, and other artistic elements. Teachers reinforce *visualization* by encouraging dancers to use their minds as well as their bodies to prepare for a performance. They may suggest mental pictures for the shy student to help her become a secure, self-confident performer. Dancers with stage fright can visualize themselves performing without fear. Those with a particular 'block' against turns, for example, can use it to dispel their anxiety. The mind is an incredible motivator.

Memory retention is likewise an essential ability for any aspiring dance student to cultivate. Teachers are directly responsible for its development, and should continually challenge students to develop it. It begins with the expectation of remembering a set of classroom exercises. Early on, after first practicing a single movement successively until it is understood and executed correctly, short sets of steps can be combined both at barre and in the center. As an artist they will be required to remember entire ballet evenings, so this skill is of vital importance. *It is important for teachers to demonstrate, but not perform these combinations of steps with the students.* Imitation is an early learning tool, but does not require students to remember on their own, which is the ultimate goal. Groups of students and lines within groups should be alternated often during a dance class to ensure that students are not depending upon others to remember the steps. In this way all students eventually perform in the front line—with no one to watch except their own image in the mirror. The added benefit to this way of teaching *memory retention* is that students develop self-confidence. At an audition, students who can quickly assimilate different combinations and styles stand out. Another way in which *memory retention* serves the student is in technical improvement. If a student is capable of remembering corrections given in class and rehearsal, both individually and to others, their skill will increase exponentially.

The last 'intangible' is that of *Imagination/Creativity*, and it lends itself to artistic performance in a number of ways. Both teachers and students draw upon their imaginations to create choreography or characters or stories to support their work. Teachers often use imagery to connect with their students: when lowering the leg to the floor they may tell students to imagine the leg is a feather floating to the ground, or that the final pose (*tendu*) places the toe upon a fragile eggshell. As students develop into artists they will use their own imaginations and give themselves imagery ideas that work for them. When teachers use imagery, their students have learned the process and can emulate it.

Imagination and *Creativity* are equally important when a performer is called upon to dance a role in a *style* that may be new to them. Ballets set in the Romantic period necessitate a different way of moving than contemporary choreography. Adapting one's technique after (perhaps) years of training in a freer, more athletic mode to an historic *style* that restricts arms to rounded poses and heads held in tilted positions (for example) can be a challenge to many dancers. Here, *artistry* separates those who merely imitate from those who 'feel' the choreographer's intention. The teacher or director should make every effort to explain consistency and earmarks of a *style*, and allow the dancers to 'grow into' an understanding of the desired way of executing movements. Mastering this takes time and patience. It is not only past eras that define different styles: individual choreographers each have their own. Balanchine's was unlike that of Robert Joffrey, and dancers moving from one company job to another may find themselves 're-created' to suit the works they perform.

Now that *The Intangibles* have been added to the dancer's knowledge, she is ready to make the transition from performer to artist. The art of dance is elusive, without the lasting immortality of creation that we associate with sculpture or writing. The ballet student is given only a short time to develop and refine a complicated set of physical abilities. It is the teacher's extended responsibility to take the student past technique whenever possible.

NOTE: This chapter information has been exerpted from my M.F.A. thesis entitled "Ballet Pedagogy: A Conceptual Approach" (M. Z. Gaston)

GLOSSARY OF TERMS

Explanation of Common Ballet Terms as Used in this Book

(For a comprehensive list and definitions of all ballet terms, please consult the "Technical Manual and Dictionary of Classical Ballet" book by Gail Grant)

1. ***changé*** versus ***sans changé***

   - *changé(e) (*changed*)* defines a step in which the feet change, meaning if the step began with the right foot front in 5th position it would end with the left foot front.
     Example: *glissade changée (*glide changed), or *échappé changé* (escaped, changed)

   - *sans changé* (without change) the opposite of *changé,* defines a step that begins and ends with the same foot front
     Example*: glissade sans changée* (glide without change)

   Note that the extra "e" added denotes a step that is feminine in gender in French

2. ***elevé* versus *relevé*** (in this book a distinction is made)

- *elevé* (rise, rising) is a term of the French school to indicate rising to the balls of the feet or to full pointe smoothly, meaning without a preceding or finishing *demi-plié*, thus with the legs straight throughout. Today this term is often not used, but it does help to distinguish between the two methods of rising so it is here still included. **Note:** the French term *élève* means "student" or "pupil" and is a different word altogether. The placement of the accents changes the pronunciation and meaning of the two words when spoken.

- *relevé* (rise, rising) is used by Cecchetti/Russian schools to indicate rising by way of a *demi-plié* to facilitate a "spring" up to the balls of the feet, or to full pointe. It is not a jump since the feet do not leave the floor.
  Example: *relevé sur les pointes* (risen to the toes)
  Example: *relevé en arabesque* (*arabesque* done while rising)

- The term *relevé* is often used for both ways to rise.

3. *en avant* versus *devant*

- *en avant* ("forward, to the front") refers to a step that moves the entire body forward.
  Example: *glissade en avant* (a glissade that travels forward)

- *devant* ("in front") refers to a step or pose placed in front of the body.
  Example: *battement tendu devant*
  Example: "step ends with R. foot *devant*" means it ends with R. foot placed in front

- Opposite terms: ***en arrière* versus *derrière***

4. *en haut* versus *en bas*

- *en haut* ("high") refers to a high position of the arm (or arms), i.e., above the head. Note that <u>this term is not used to refer to positions of the legs.</u>
  Example: 5th position *en haut* (French or Cecchetti port de bras position)

- Opposite term: *en bas* (low)

5. *passé* versus *retiré*

- The term *passé r*efers to the *retiré* position when it is used as a "pass-through" to reach another position.
  Example: the initial movement of a *développé,* or by picking up the working leg from 5th position in front and then closing it behind in 5th position.

- The term *retiré* here refers to the "withdrawn" position in which one leg is bent at the knee and drawn into the standing leg so that the toe is placed in front, behind, or beside the supporting knee.
  Example: *retiré devant* (the position above with the toe placed in front of the knee, the standard position for most pirouettes)

6. *plié* versus *fondu*

- *plié* ("bent, bending") In English we use the word "pliable" to describe something that is "bendable." In ballet, a *plié* refers to bending <u>both legs</u>, for our purposes.
  Example: *demi-plié* or half-bend

- *fondu(e)* ("melted") is to one leg what *plié* is to two legs—besides being a specific barre exercise (*battement fondu*), it can be used to describe any pose or movement in which the standing leg is bent.
  Example: *arabesque fondue* (because the term *arabesque* is feminine, the descriptive word much match in gender, thus the "e" on the end of the word *fondu*)

7. *sauté* versus *temps levé*

- *Sauté* (jumped or jumping) describes a movement done while jumping.
  Example: *échappé sauté*

- *Temps levé* ("time raised" Cecchetti term) refers specifically to a hop on one foot that lands on that same foot
  Example: *temps levé en arabesque* (a hop on one foot with the working leg in *arabesque*)

8. working leg, standing leg, supporting leg

- Working leg refers to the leg executing a movement and not bearing the body weight

- Standing leg or supporting leg refers to the leg bearing the body weight

REFERENCE SHEET 1

In this book, directions (such as "corner 1" etc.) refer to: **Cecchetti "fixed points" (reference points)** of studio or stage space as seen below.

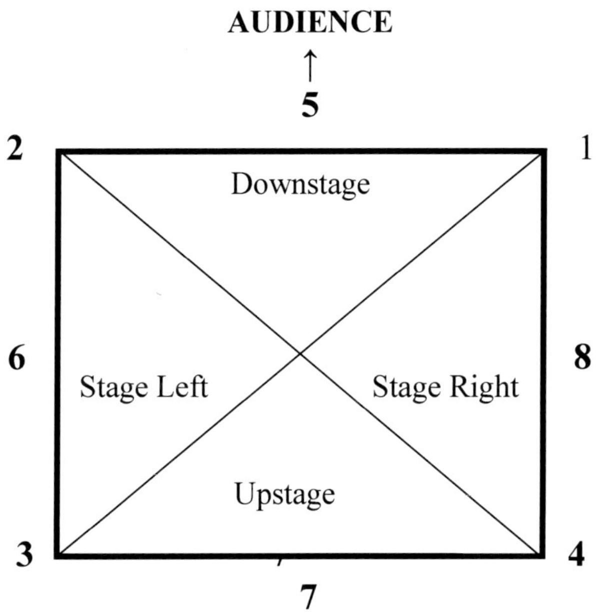

Center stage is at the intersection point of the two diagonal lines. "Downstage center" would then indicate a dancer standing near the number "5" above.

NOTE: Vaganova fixed points differ—this book refers most often to Cecchetti

It is customary for Stage Left moving dancers to cross in front of dancers coming from Stage Right in choreographic patterns unless the choreographer specifies otherwise.

REFERENCE SHEET 2

Photographic References to Body Positions Used in this Book (Cecchetti)

Croisé devant

À la quatrième devant

Écarté

Effacé

À la seconde

Épaulé

À la quatrième derrière

Croisé derrière

More body positions, Vaganova:

Éffacé derrière

Écarté derrière

Épaulé derrière

Note these differences between Cecchetti (on L.) and Vaganova body positions:

Croisé derrière (arms & head)

◄

Additionally, there are often minor differences in arm and head in other poses—for example, arms held in second tend to be held higher in Vaganova than in Cecchetti positions.

In *écarté* body position, the body is tilted slightly away from the working leg and the head held with chin slightly raised (tilted upward), as opposed to Cecchetti, in which the position is directly centered over the supporting leg with the head held straighter.

REFERENCE SHEET 3

Photographic Reference to Arm Positions (Various numbering and terminology of Port de bras positions used by different methods)

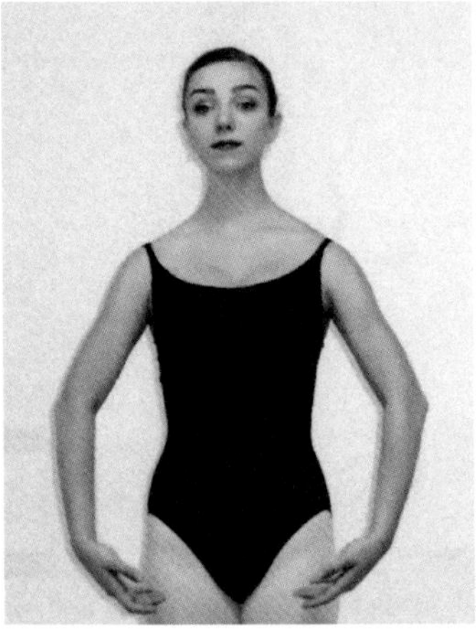

First (with feet in first) or **Fifth *en bas*** (with feet in 5th (Cecchetti) OR **Bras au repos** (French) OR **Preparatory position** (Russian) ▲

First (French & Russian) OR **Fifth *en avant*** (Cecchetti) ▲

Second position (all methods)

Demi-seconde
(Cecchetti)

Third (Cecchetti) with
feet in 3rd

Third (French) OR
Fourth *en haut* (Cecchetti)
with feet in 4th position
croisée

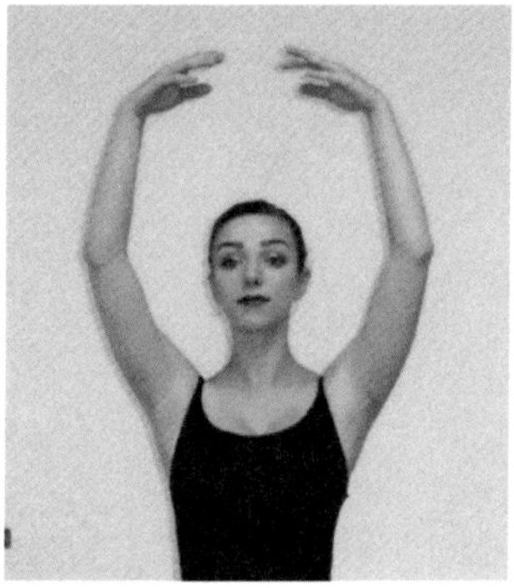

Third (Russian)
OR
Fifth (French) OR
Fifth en haut (with
feet in 5th
(Cecchetti)

Fourth (French)

Fourth en avant (Cecchetti) with feet in 4th position *croisée*

Head positions

Five principal positions of the head (Cecchetti):

Erect

Inclined (either side)

Turned (either side)

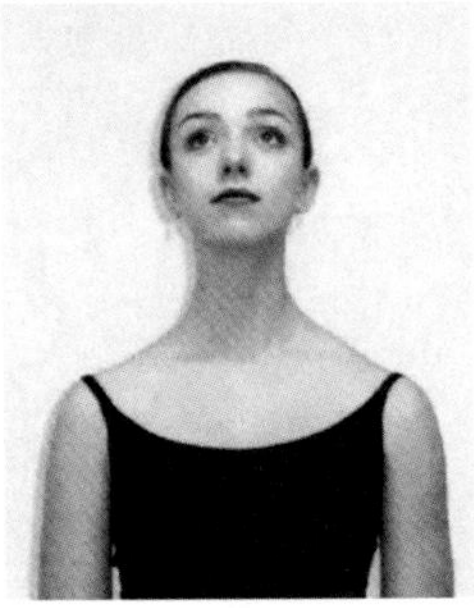

Raised

Lowered

Some head position possibilities when working at the barre.

Usual rules: head turns away from working leg in *à la seconde* when traveling backwards (away from audience), and vice versa. Head remains in position as foot closes in 5th.

REFERENCE SHEET 4

Arabesque and Attitude Positions

1st Arabesque (Cecchetti) ▲

1st Arabesque (Vaganova) ▼ (R. arm slightly more forward)

2nd Arabesque (Cecchetti)

2nd Arabesque (Vaganova)

3rd Arabesque, Cecchetti ▲

3rd Arabesque, Vaganova

◀

4th Arabesque, Cecchetti ▲

4th Arabesque, Vaganova ◄

5th
Arabesque
,Cecchetti)

◀

1st
Arabesque
penchée

◀

Attitude Positions:

Attitude effacée (Cecchetti on L., Vaganova on R.)

Attitude croisée derrière (Cecchetti on L., Vaganova on R.)

Attitude épaulée

Attitude croisée devant

Attitude
croisée
derrière,
penchée

◄

ACKNOWLEDGEMENTS

This is my fourth ballet book, devoted to teachers everywhere who want to expand and explore new ideas in the field of teaching pointe. It is such a broad subject and yet one that demands specific knowledge beyond just teaching ballet.

Some say that pointe work is almost self-taught, yet clearly there is a difference of ability among those students who are left "on their own" to convert their prior training into pointe work and those who have had careful mentoring by an accomplished teacher who has, herself, experienced advanced-level pointe work both onstage and off.

Sharing our knowledge enhances it, and widens our horizons. Teaching is really a way to learn more from others and pass on what others gave to us. The key word in teaching pointe is preparation. Without it a student approaches it blindly and may find it so daunting that it defeats her just at the time when she is on the threshold of developing into a performing artist.

My first ballet book on teaching (*Building Ballet Technique: A Practical Guide for Teaching All Levels*) and the second book *(Building Ballet Technique: A Self-Improvement Guide for Dancers*) were written to satisfy two needs that I felt had not been addressed sufficiently in other writings on the subjects: one was for a step-by-step, organized way to present teaching material that linked together and progressed in a logical way that covered all levels aimed at both neophyte and experienced teachers, and the second book's theme was to answer many of the questions that students often have about their own personal technical problems, and present possible solutions for them. The third book, *Building Ballet Technique: 110*

Progressive Teaching Combinations for All Levels, Center Floor was a reiteration of my belief that teaching through a "stepping stone" approach is both valid and productive and results in consistently achieving students.

As usual, I owe a debt of gratitude to Mrs. Edith L. Clark, A.R.A.D., a dear friend and accomplished teacher. We talk often, share ideas, and compare notes about students, teaching methods, and other ballet-related topics, and that informal input often helps me develop new throughts when I write.

Likewise, of course, I have had the very fortunate chance to study with excellent teachers and dancers over the years, and perform as a professional in ballet companies—and all of that knowledge and exposure lent itself to my teaching later in life, in countless, priceless ways. Along the way I gathered ideas from as many sources as I could, and continue to do so. It's a never-ending but very gratifying process.

My devoted students keep me sane in every sense—they not only inspire, they never cease to change and develop, yet over the years they remain basically the same—reminding me of when I, too, "lived, ate, and slept" ballet. Thank you all for keeping the love of dance alive and well.

And as I said in my last book's acknowledgements, I never thought anything in my life would ever be as difficult as becoming a professional dancer—a goal which took me many years and much hard work to accomplish. I was wrong! Writing about dance is equally challenging. Now, in addition to putting steps in order, I put words in order. Instead (and along with) rehearsing choreography, I proofread. And just as with dancing, we all sometimes make mistakes. If I've made any in this book, editorially, typographically, grammatically or otherwise, I take full responsibility. This is entirely my own work, though of course there are some thoughts that are so universal with any subject that they may coincide with others; if so, it was completely unintentional.

PHOTO CREDITS

THE MODELS (all are students at the Orlando Ballet School, Orlando, Florida):

Audrey Perryman

Elisabeth Regault

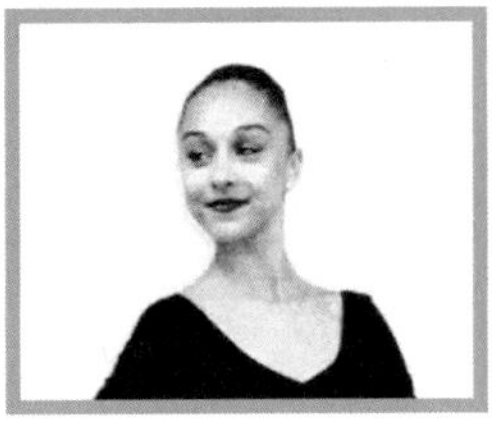

Angelina Broad

Evangeline Bell-Cotter

Nathalie Friederich

Sophia McFadden

Leanna Wagner

Cover photo of Leanna Wagner

Photography by Marilyn Gaston

My sincere thanks to the Orlando Ballet School for use of their facilities and students for the photography.

ABOUT THE AUTHOR

Marilyn Z. Gaston began her professional performing career before and after graduation with a B.F.A. in Ballet/Theatre from Texas Christian University. She danced with the Ft. Worth Ballet, Casa Mañana Summer Musicals, Inc., the Atlanta Ballet Company from 1972-74 and, from 1974-1977 she was engaged as a fully-contracted company member with the German State Theatre ballet companies in Lübeck and Karlsrühe (Germany), and the Ballet du Rhin (then housed in Strasbourg, France). She later also danced with the professional company of the Maryland Ballet when it was headquartered in Baltimore until 1979.

Upon returning to the U.S. from Europe, Ms. Gaston began teaching in universities, private dance schools and pre-professional studios. In 1981 she founded the Ballet Academy of Baltimore and the Ballet Concerto of Baltimore, now known collectively as the Baltimore Ballet, and continued in that capacity for 17 years, until 1997. She served on the dance faculties of Towson University, Goucher College, Loyola University (Baltimore), Tyler Jr. College (Texas), and other universities, and later completed a Master of Fine Arts degree in Dance (ballet emphasis) on a teaching fellowship in 2012 at the University of Oklahoma. Her past students have been accepted into college dance programs, pre-professional schools, and professional dance companies. Recently she was certified by the American Ballet Theatre National Teacher Training Program for levels Pre-Primary through Level 3 as the first part of completion of all the levels in the future.

In 2008 Ms. Gaston completed an M.F.A. in Creative Writing at Queens University of Charlotte. She has two fiction books (under M.Z. Gaston), and three other ballet books in this series in publication. She currently teaches at the Orlando Ballet School, Florida.

66739723R10090

Made in the USA
Lexington, KY
22 August 2017